THE POLITICS OF THE VEIL

THE PUBLIC SQUARE BOOK SERIES

PRINCETON UNIVERSITY PRESS

Ruth O'Brien, *Series Editor*

THE POLITICS OF THE VEIL

Joan Wallach Scott

PRINCETON UNIVERSITY PRESS ◻ *Princeton and Oxford*

Copyright © 2007 by Princeton University Press

Published by Princeton University Press, 41 William Street,
Princeton, New Jersey 08540

In the United Kingdom: Princeton University Press, 6 Oxford Street,
Woodstock, Oxfordshire OX20 1TW

press.princeton.edu

Eighth printing, and first paperback printing, 2010
Paperback ISBN: 978-0-691-14798-7

THE LIBRARY OF CONGRESS HAS CATALOGED THE CLOTH EDITION
OF THIS BOOK AS FOLLOWS
Scott, Joan Wallach.
The politics of the veil / Joan Wallach Scott.
p. cm. — (The public square)
Includes bibliographical references and index.
ISBN-13: 978-0-691-12543-5 (hardcover : alk. paper)
1. Muslims—France. 2. Islamophobia—France. 3. Racism—France.
4. Hijab (Islamic clothing)—Law and legislation—France.   5. Muslims—
Cultural assimilation—France.   6. Secularism—France.
7. Culture conflict—France.   I. Title.
DC34.5.M87S36 2007
305.6′970944—dc22   2007013953

British Library Cataloging-in-Publication Data is available

This book has been composed in Adobe Caslon and Helvetica Neue

Printed on acid-free paper. ∞

Printed in the United States of America

11 12 13 14 15 16 17 18 19 20

CONTENTS

FOREWORD

Convening in a church's basement daycare center, a British Christian group holds a "how to" workshop on heckling Muslims who lecture in London's Hyde Park Speakers Corner. After hearing that half the Dutch Muslims don't speak the language, the Parliament of the Netherlands, a country known for centuries of religious and political tolerance, debates whether such individuals should be compelled to take Dutch language classes. And in the German Bundestag, politicians contemplate forbidding imams from preaching in Arabic. But it is in France where public protest and government sanctions against Muslims first took hold.

In her compelling book *The Politics of the Veil*, Joan Wallach Scott points out that France initiated the discussion in the late 1980s about prohibiting public school girls from wearing headscarves. This discussion culminated in 2004 with such a ban. Two years later, the French government made it illegal to deny that the Turkish killing of Armenians between 1915 and 1917 was genocide.

These sanctions have inflamed rather than eliminated the extremism that led to the commuter-train bombings in Madrid by a Moroccan terrorist cell in 2003; the murder of Dutch filmmaker Theo van Gogh, allegedly by a Dutch-Moroccan Muslim radical in 2004; and the bombs that exploded in London in 2005. Indeed, moderate Muslim groups are beginning to portray Europe as a "closed Christian club," and 80 percent of Muslims now feel harassed and discriminated against, a figure that has grown from 35 percent just seven years ago. That many Muslims feel "under siege" only further fosters an environment ripe for extremism.

Meanwhile, fundamentalist Muslims use these bans to galvanize their own forces. Al-Qaeda's number two in command, Ayman Al-Zawahiri, lashed out at "those in France who prevent Muslims from covering their heads in schools." When the sanction first took effect, protests broke out on streets from Rabat to Jakarta. In the view of Muslims around the globe, the French law was a deliberate attack on six million of its own residents—the largest Muslim community in Europe. Later, the riots by French youth, primarily of Algerian and Moroccan colonial descent, expressed widespread feelings of bias, prejudice, and betrayal.

Recognizing that the symbolism of the headscarf ban ignites the anti-immigration Muslim crisis in Europe, the European Union (EU) commissioned a three-year study entitled the VEIL, an acronym for Values, Equality and Differences in Liberal Democracies. It focuses on Austria, Denmark, France, Greece, Germany, Turkey, the Netherlands, and the United Kingdom, and is charged with evaluating the range of anti-discrimination policies and strategies that exist to better integrate minorities, particularly Muslim women, into the European community.

The EU is, however, anything but consistent. Nor is the European Council. In 1998, the European Court of Human Rights upheld Turkey's headscarf ban in public buildings, calling it "a victory for Ankara's secularists after a long legal bat-

tle." The court in Strasbourg confirmed an earlier ruling that
barred a woman from taking a university exam because she
wore a headscarf.

The West has long encouraged the secularization of the
East. According to Scott, the notion that banning headscarves
represents modernization should be challenged. For many in
France the fight about secularism is a means (Scott calls it a
cover-up) by which the differences between the East and West,
Islam and liberal values are accentuated. This is a fight to define the borders of Europe. But, as Scott so convincingly argues, the polemic hides a more complex reality. There is no ei-
ther/or. The struggle is not between tradition and modernity.
Nor is it about presumably universalist values such as the separation of church and state. It is a controversy that reveals the
prejudices that white Judeo-Christian Europeans harbor
against a portion of their nation's denizens, many of whose
parents and grandparents came from their former colonies.
Laws banning the Islamic headscarf, Scott argues, are fueled by
racism, post-colonial guilt and fear, and nationalism.

What is more, the latest policies exacerbate ethnic and religious differences. Most Muslims in France describe themselves
first as French and second as practitioners of Islam. Scott's
book brings us to the Public Square by showing the effects of
laws such as the headscarf prohibition. Islamic nonprofit
groups predict the law will simply lead to a boom in private
Muslim education, sharpening the very divisions it was intended to fight. *The Politics of the Veil* starkly reveals the linea-
ments of the crisis European nations face as they incorporate
their immigrant populations, many of them from former
colonies, many of them Muslims, into what were once taken to

be largely homogeneous societies. Scott's book shows us that
this crisis is anything but simple and that there are voices proposing alternate solutions to legal prohibition. This gives us
ample room for the kind of debate that should occur in the
public square.

RUTH O'BRIEN
The CUNY Graduate Center
New York, New York

ACKNOWLEDGMENTS

Without the encouragement of Ruth O'Brien and Brigitta van Rheinberg, what began as a lecture would never have turned into a book. I am grateful that they invited me to undertake this project and for their enthusiastic support along the way. Although I had clear opinions about the headscarf ban from the beginning, it took a lot of thought to formulate them; there are sections of the book that I rewrote several times in response to criticism from colleagues and friends. For their objections, advice, and suggestions I would like to thank Talal Asad, Beth Baron, Patrick Chabal, Brian Connolly, Eric Fassin, Kristen Chodsee, David Scott, Donald Scott, Tony Scott, Farzana Shaikh, Lisa Weedeen, and Elizabeth Weed. Françoise Gaspard and Claude Servan-Schreiber offered many important corrections, as well as clarifications about French history and politics, though I don't think they always shared my point of view. Wendy Brown read the first version of the entire manuscript and forced me to re-think some of its argument. When Saba Mahmood read a later version, her comments prompted yet another revision. The members of the Yale Law Theory Workshop pushed me hard on questions about secularism, as did the members of the "'Third World' Now" seminar in the School of Social Science at the Institute for Advanced Study. What appears here is a lot better than those earlier drafts thanks to their interventions.

In any research and writing I've undertaken, the support of the staff at the Institute for Advanced Study has been invaluable. Thanks especially to librarian Marcia Tucker, to Donne Petito, and to my assistant, Nancy Cotterman, problem-solvers *par excellence.*

The most important debt I have at the Institute is a long-term one, and it is, in a way, too late to acknowledge it. During more than twenty years on the faculty of the Institute, I learned most from my late colleague Clifford Geertz. He might have found this book too strong an argument for his taste, but I think he would have appreciated its intention: to make sense of a set of events beyond their literal representation and to take a position that, as he once put it, was "a thorn in the side of the main direction of things." Cliff enabled many of us in the Institute's School of Social Science to enact that motto and it has made a tremendous difference, not only in our own work, but in the disciplines to which we are attached. In gratitude for his intellectual and institutional leadership and for his friendship, I dedicate this book to the memory of Clifford Geertz.

THE POLITICS OF THE VEIL

INTRODUCTION

On March 15, 2004, the French government passed a law that banned the wearing of "conspicuous signs" of religious affiliation in public schools. Article 1 is the key provision:

> In public elementary, middle and high schools, the wearing of signs or clothing which conspicuously manifest students' religious affiliations is prohibited. Disciplinary procedures to implement this rule will be preceded by a discussion with the student.

There is also an explanation of what counts as "conspicuous":

> The clothing and religious signs prohibited are conspicuous signs such as a large cross, a veil, or a skullcap. Not regarded as signs indicating religious affiliation are discreet signs, which can be, for example, medallions, small crosses, stars of David, hands of Fatima, or small Korans.

Although the law applied to Jewish boys in skullcaps and Sikh boys in turbans, as well as to anyone with a large cross around his or her neck, it was aimed primarily at Muslim girls wearing headscarves (*hijab* in Arabic; *foulard* in French). The other groups were included to undercut the charge of discrimination against Muslims and to comply with a requirement that such laws apply universally. The headscarf, or, as it was soon to be referred to almost exclusively, the veil (*voile*), was considered inimical to French custom and law because it violated the separation of church and state, insisted on differences among citizens in a nation one and indivisible, and accepted the subordination of women in a republic premised on equality. For many supporters of the law, the veil was the ultimate symbol of Islam's resistance to modernity.

France is not the only country to worry about girls or women in headscarves. Similar legislation has been proposed in Belgium, Australia, Holland, and Bulgaria. In Turkey, which presents a different set of issues—a secular state since 1923 (modeled on the French republic), it has a majority Muslim population—a ban applies to elected officials, civil servants, and school and university students. In Bulgaria, which has long had a significant Muslim minority, a law to prohibit headscarves is still being discussed, but its proponents seem driven at least in part by a desire to be acceptable "Europeans." In Germany, most of whose Muslims come from Turkey, many regional states prohibit teachers (though not students) from wearing the hijab. The European Court of Human Rights has weighed in on the matter too, ruling in a Turkish case that governments are within their rights when they prohibit headscarves in schools. This ruling is meant to apply to all European countries, not only to Turkey. A dissenting note has been sounded by the UN committee charged with implementing CEDAW (the convention outlawing all forms of discrimination against women): in 2005, it expressed concern about the effects of such bans on women's access to schools and universities. Still, there seems to be a consensus about the meaning of the headscarf and the challenge to secular democracy that it represents, even though the girls and adult women who wear them are decidedly a minority within diasporic Muslim populations.

Indeed, the numbers do not explain the attention being paid to veils. In France, just before the law was passed, only 14 percent of Muslim women polled wore the hijab, although 51 percent declared that they actively practiced their religion.[1] In the Netherlands, which proposed outlawing the *burqa* (the full-body covering worn by women), it is estimated that only fifty to one hundred women wear it, out of a population of about a million Muslims.[2] Similarly, in England, where the *niqab*, which covers a woman's entire face except for her eyes, was the focus of controversy in 2006, the number of wearers is tiny, though BBC news reported an increase in sales of niqabs in reaction to ex–foreign secretary Jack Straw's proposal to ban them. Banning the headscarf or veil is a symbolic gesture; for some European nations it is a way of taking a stand against Islam, declaring entire Muslim populations to be a threat to national integrity and harmony. The radical acts of a few politically inspired Islamists have become a declaration of the intent of the many; the religious practices of minorities have been taken to stand for the "culture" of the whole, and the notion of a fixed Muslim "culture" obscures the mixed sociological realities of adaptation and discrimination experienced by these immigrants to the West.

My question in this book is, why the headscarf? What is it about the headscarf that makes it the focus of controversy, the sign of something intolerable? The simple answers offered by

politicians who pass the laws and some feminists who support
them is that the veil is an emblem of radical Islamist politics.
In the words of the Australian Brownyn Bishop, "it has become the icon, the symbol of the clash of cultures, and it runs
much deeper than a piece of cloth." In addition, it is widely argued that veils stand for the oppression of women. So insists
Margaret De Cuyper of Holland: "Women have lived for too
long with clothes and standards decided for them by men; this
[the removal of the veil] is a victory."[3]

These answers don't explain enough. Headscarves (or veils)
are worn by only a small fraction of Muslim women, the vast
majority of whom have assimilated in some way or another to
the Western values and dress of the countries in which they
now live. Moreover, veils are not the only visible sign of difference that attaches to religious Muslims, not the only way a re-
ligious/political identity can be declared. Men often have distinctive appearances (beards, loose clothing) and behavior
(prayers, food preferences, aggressive assertions of religious
identity tied to activist politics), yet these are not considered to
be as threatening as the veil and so are not addressed by legal
prohibition. The laws do not go on to challenge the structures
of gender inequality in codes of Muslim family law; these
codes have been allowed to stand in some Western European
countries, and are left to religious authorities to enforce, even if
they are not the law of the host country. Even more confound-
ing, concern with gender inequality seems limited to Muslims
and does not extend to French or German or Dutch practices
that also permit the subordination of women. It is as if patriarchy were a uniquely Islamic phenomenon!

What is it about the status of women in Islam that invites

special remedial attention? Why has the veil been singled out as an icon of the intolerable difference of Muslims? How has insistence on the political significance of the veil obscured other anxieties and concerns of those obsessed with it? How has the veil become a way of addressing broad issues of ethnicity and integration in France and in Western Europe more generally? To answer these questions we cannot take at face value the simple oppositions offered by those who would ban it: traditional versus modern, fundamentalism versus secularism, church versus state, private versus public, particular versus universal, group versus individual, cultural pluralism versus national unity, identity versus equality. These dichotomies do not capture the complexities of either Islam or "the West." Rather, they are polemics that in fact create their own reality: incompatible cultures, a clash of civilizations.

A number of studies argue convincingly that the Islamic headscarf is a modern, not a traditional, phenomenon, an effect of recent geopolitical and cultural exchanges that are global in scale. The French sociologist Olivier Roy, for example, describes the current religiosity of Muslim populations in Europe as both a product of and a reaction to westernization. The new Islamic religiosity, he maintains, parallels similar quests for new forms of spirituality in the secular environments of the West. "Islam," he writes, "cannot escape the New Age of religion or choose the form of its own modernity."[4] I would add that while present-day Islam is undeniably "modern," there is not one universalizing form of its modernity, and it is especially the differences that matter. I agree with Roy that today's Islam is not a throwback to earlier practices, nor does it emanate from bounded traditions or identifiable communities.

There is not, Roy insists, a single Muslim "culture" which corresponds to the sociological and demographic profiles of the immigrant populations now residing in Europe. Indeed Islam is historically decentralized; unlike Catholicism, with its headquarters in Rome and a single figure of authority at its head, Islamic theology is articulated through continuing debate and interpretation, much like Jewish theology. Moreover, there is no single theology, but a plurality of them. Among Muslim immigrant populations, there are, to be sure, attempts to establish group identifications, but these are voluntary, Roy says, since they do not correspond any longer to fixed places—territories, states—or even to institutions like the family. In fact, voluntary groupings tend to divide generations; religiosity is one way for children to declare their independence from family constraints. It is also a way for dominated groups to insist on the legitimacy of their religion. The contexts within which populations assert Islamic identity need to be specified. What does establish Muslims as a single community, a "virtual" community in Roy's description of it, is "specific legislation" that serves to "objectify" them.[5] Various judicial and legislative decrees in Western Europe, prominently among them the French law banning Islamic headscarves, are examples of this objectification.

The intense debates about passing such laws serve another purpose as well: they offer a defense of the European nation-states at a moment of crisis. As membership in the European Union threatens national sovereignty (borders, passports, currency, finance) and calls for an overhaul of social policy (the welfare state, labor market regulation, gender relations), as globalization weakens the standing of domestic markets, and as former colonial subjects seek a permanent place in the metropole, the question of national identity has loomed large in Western Europe. Depending on particular national histories, the idealization of the nation has taken various forms. In France it has taken the form of an insistence on the values and beliefs of the republic, said to be a realization of the principles of the Enlightenment in their highest, most enduring form. This image of France is mythical; its power and appeal rests, to a large degree, on its negative portrayal of Islam. The objectification of Muslims as a fixed "culture" has its counterpart in the mythologizing of France as an enduring "republic." Both are imagined to lie outside history—antagonists locked in eternal combat.

This dual construction, France versus its Muslims, is an operation in virtual community building. It is the result of a sustained polemic, a political *discourse*. I understand discourse to refer to interpretation, to the imposition of meaning on phenomena in the world; it is mutable and contested, and so the stakes are high. Discourse is an important way of characterizing what I am studying; I use the term to counter the notion of culture that was employed in the debates. Culture in those usages implied objectively discernible values and traditions that were homogeneous and immutable; complexity, politics, and history were absent. Culture was said to be the *cause* of the differences between France and its Muslims. In fact, I argue that this idea of culture was the *effect* of a very particular, historically specific political discourse. Creating the reality one wants requires strong argument and the discrediting, if not silencing, of alternative points of view. Outlawing the veil, even though it was worn by very few students in French public schools, was an attempt to enact a particular version of reality, one which insisted on assimilation as the only way for Muslims to become French. The presentation of what it meant to be "French" required suppressing not only the critics who were themselves French (and not Muslim) but also the Muslims (many of whom were French citizens) who offered conflicting evidence about the meanings of their religious identifications and of the place of the headscarf in them.

The study of political discourse is best undertaken through close readings of arguments advanced in their specific political and historical contexts. Without history we aren't able to grasp the implications of the ideas being advanced; we don't hear the resonances of words; we don't see all of the symbols contained——for example——in a piece of cloth that serves as a veil. For that reason this book is centered on the politics of headscarf controversies in France—a country whose history I have been studying for almost forty years. There are, of course, insights I offer that have more general application. These insights are based on my belief that we need to recognize and negotiate differences, even those that seem irreducible—an outlook many French commentators would dismiss as American and multiculturalist (synonymous in their view). To be sure, my ideas are an expression of my political outlook, but it's not so much an American way of thinking as it is a particular understanding of what democracy requires in the present context. There are many Americans who do not share my views, just as there is a significant minority in France, many of whom I cite in the course of this book, who do share them.

These reflections about processes of politics and the handling of differences are not confined to national contexts; they have wider application. The objectification of Muslims; the attribution of their differences to a single, inassimilable culture; the idea that a secular way of life is being threatened by "fundamentalists"—all this is evident in the reaction of Western European leaders to Muslim immigrants in their midst. Still, the specific ways in which these ideas are expressed and implemented as policy differ according to national political histories. These histories are critical for our understanding of the "Muslim problem" in Europe. For that reason I have confined my analyses to France, not only to gain the depth this issue requires, but also to highlight the local nature of the imagined general conflict between "Islam" and "the West." It is, of course, true that there is a global dimension to these conflicts, the more so as the Middle East becomes a central strategic concern of American foreign policy, *the* site for the enduring "war against terrorism," and as identification with a transnational Islam becomes the basis for rallying political opposition to the West in general and to the United States in particular. But, I argue, the situation of Muslim immigrants in Western European countries can be fully grasped only if the local context is taken into account. So, for example, a nation's policy for naturalizing immigrants plays a part in its reception of Muslims; the experience of Pakistanis in England differs from that of Algerians in France; that of Turks in Germany is different yet again, while Bulgaria's Muslims are not immigrants at all. We don't learn very much by lumping all of these cases together into one Muslim "problem." In fact, we exacerbate the problem we seek to address. I think that exactly this kind of heightening of difficulties was produced in France by the ways in which politicians, public intellectuals, and the media responded to the fact of a growing population of Muslim "immigrants" in their midst—immigrants whose diversities were reduced to a single difference that was then taken to be a threat to the very identity of the nation.

This book is a study of the political discourse of those French republicans who insisted that the only way to deal with what they perceived to be the threat of Islamic separatism was to ban the headscarf. There are not many Muslim voices in this book, in part because there weren't many to be heard during the debates. The headscarf controversies were largely an affair of those who defined themselves as representatives of a true France, with North Africans, Muslims, and "immigrants" consigned to the periphery. I do consider the many meanings the veil may have for Muslims and arguments among them about how and whether to assimilate to French standards, but only briefly and then as a way of highlighting the inconsistencies of French characterizations of them. *This is not a book about French Muslims; it is about the dominant French view of them.* I am interested in the way in which the veil became a screen onto which were projected images of strangeness and fantasies of danger—danger to the fabric of French society and to the future of the republican nation. I am also interested in the way in which the representation of a homogeneous and dangerous "other" secured a mythic vision of the French republic, one and indivisible. I explore the many factors feeding these fantastic representations: racism, postcolonial guilt and fear, and nationalist ideologies, including republicanism, secularism, abstract individualism, and, especially, French norms of sexual conduct taken to be both natural and universal. Indeed, I argue that the representation of Muslim sexuality as unnatural and oppressive when compared to an imagined French way of doing sex intensified objections to the veil, grounding these in indisputable moral and psychological conviction.

✦

In France many of those who supported a ban on headscarves insisted they were protecting a nation conceived to be one and indivisible from the corrosive effects of *communautarisme* (which I have translated as "communalism"). By that term, they do not mean exactly what Americans do by "communitarianism." In France *communautarisme* refers to the priority of group over national identity in the lives of individuals; in theory there is no possibility of a hyphenated ethnic/national identity—one belongs either to a group or to the nation. (In fact, of course, there are French Muslims who were recognized as such at the end of the Algerian War, but that history was conveniently forgotten in the outburst of republican myth making associated with the celebration of the bicentennial of the French Revolution in 1989.) American multiculturalism was offered negatively as the embodiment of communalism. Consisting of a multiplicity of cultures, riven by ethnic conflict and group identity politics, the United States is depicted as unable to grant individuals the equality that is their natural right. That equality is achieved, in French political theory, by making one's social, religious, ethnic, and other origins irrelevant in the public sphere; it is as an abstract individual that one becomes a French citizen. Universalism—the oneness, the sameness of all individuals—is taken to be the antithesis of communalism. And yet, paradoxically, it is a universalism that is particularly

French. If America permits the coexistence of many cultures and grants the legitimacy (and political influence) of hyphenated identities (Italian-American, Irish-American, African-American, etc.), France insists on assimilation to a singular culture, the embrace of a shared language, history, and political ideology. The ideology is French republicanism. Its hallmarks are secularism and individualism, the linked concepts that guarantee all individuals equal protection by the state against the claims of religion and any other group demands.

French universalism insists that sameness is the basis for equality. To be sure, sameness is an abstraction, a philosophical notion meant to achieve the formal equality of individuals before the law. But historically it has been applied literally: assimilation means the eradication of difference. That is why the French census makes no record of the religion, ethnicity, or national origin of its population; such figures would represent France as fractured and divided, not—as it claims to be—a united, singular entity. The ideal of a nation one and indivisible harkens back to the French Revolution of 1789, which (after several years of bloody conflict) replaced a feudal corporate regime, characterized by hierarchies of privilege based on birth and wealth, with a republic whose citizens were deemed free and equal individuals. At the time, not all members of the population were considered individuals—women and slaves lacked the requisite qualities—but the ideal stood and became part of the national heritage, inspiring the claims of excluded groups for equal rights. I will talk more about the dilemma faced by excluded *groups* claiming the rights of *individuals* in chapters 2 and 4. Here I want simply to underscore the idea that French individualism achieves its universalist status by positing the sameness of all individuals, a sameness that is achieved not simply by swearing allegiance to the nation but by assimilating to the norms of its culture. The norms of the culture, of course, are anything but abstract, and this has been the sticking point of French republican theory. Abstraction allows individuals to be conceived as the same (as universal), but sameness is measured in terms of concrete ways of being (as Frenchness). And ascriptions of difference, conceived as irreducible differences, whether based on culture or sex or sexuality, are taken to preclude any aspiration to sameness. If one has already been labeled different on any of these grounds, it is difficult to find a way of arguing that one is or can become the same.

In the last two decades or so, this contradiction has been exposed and challenged. The requirement of assimilation has come under attack by groups demanding recognition of their difference. Since women, homosexuals, and people of North African origin (stubbornly referred to as immigrants long after many had become citizens) were discriminated against as groups, it was as groups, they argued, that they must receive their rights—or as individuals whose difference from the norm is acknowledged and respected. The leaders of the feminist *mouvement pour la parité* insisted that discrimination against women in politics would end only when it was understood that all individuals came in one of two sexes. Sex, unlike ethnicity or religion, they argued, was universal. It divided all humans and so could not be abstracted: even abstract individuals were sexed. These feminists called for (and won) a law requiring equal numbers of women and men on the ballots for most elected political offices. The leaders of the gay and lesbian movement demanded the same rights for homosexual as for straight couples, including the right to be considered families. They gained the equivalent of our domestic partnership contracts, but not access to adoption or reproductive technology. In effect, the law implies that families can be formed only by two individuals of the opposite sex—the cultural norm of the heterosexual nuclear family must remain in place. North Africans, many of whom are Muslims, claimed that the only way to reverse discrimination against them was to consider their religion on a par with that of Christians and Jews. If individuals with those commitments could be considered fully French, so could Muslims, even if the requirements of their religious beliefs led them to pray and dress differently—women wearing hijabs, for example. There was, of course, great contest about what these beliefs entailed, including whether the Koran even required women to cover their heads. There was also disagreement about the wisdom of passing a law banning the foulard; many Muslims told pollsters they did not oppose such a law even as they protested the discrimination they felt it would encourage. But whatever the controversies were among Muslims, what united them as a group was the desire to be considered "fully French" without having to give up on the religious beliefs, communal ties, or other forms of behavior by which they variously identified themselves.

The reaction of politicians and republican ideologists to these demands for the recognition of difference was swift and uncompromising. They insisted that the way things had always been done was the right way and that the challenges from groups such as women, homosexuals, and immigrants would undermine the coherence and unity of the nation, betraying its revolutionary heritage. Even as they granted that discrimination might exist and allowed some measures to correct it, they did so in ways that would not endanger the bottom line: the need to maintain the unity of the nation by refusing to recognize difference. After much debate, it was established that the exception was sexual difference. Embodied in the nuclear family, it was considered to be a natural difference, the foundation not only of French culture but of all civilized cultures.

As for Muslims, their claims were rebuffed on the ground that satisfying them would undermine *laïcité*, the French version of secularism, which its apologists offer as so uniquely French as to be untranslatable. Any word has specific connotations according to its linguistic context, of course. Nevertheless, laïcité, the French version of "secularism," is no less translatable than any other term. It is part of the mythology of the specialness and superiority of French republicanism—the same mythology that paradoxically offers French universalism as different from all others—to insist that laïcité can only be used in its original tongue.[6] Laïcité means the separation of church and state through the state's protection of individuals from the claims of religion. (In the United States, in contrast, secularism connotes the protection of religions from interference by the state.) Muslim headscarves were taken to be a violation of French secularism and, by implication, a sign of the inherent non-Frenchness of anyone who practiced Islam, in whatever form. To be acceptable, religion must be a private matter; it must not be displayed "conspicuously" in public places, especially in schools, the place where the inculcation of republican ideals began. The ban on headscarves established the intention of legislators to keep France a unified nation: secular, individualist, and culturally homogeneous. They vehemently denied the objection that cultural homogeneity might also be racist. Yet, as I show in chapter 2, there is a long history of French racism in which North African Muslims are the target. The veil plays a particularly important part in that story.

One of the fascinating aspects of the headscarf controversy was the way in which words became conflated with one another. Muslim women in France wear what they refer to as a hijab; in French the word is foulard; in English, headscarf. Very quickly, this head covering was referred to in the media as a veil (voile), with the implications that the entire body and face of its wearer were hidden from view.[7] As I will argue in chapter 5, the conflation of headscarf and veil, the persistent reference to hidden faces when, in fact, they were perfectly visible, was a way of expressing deep anxiety about the ways in which Islam is understood to handle the relations of the sexes. It was also a way of insisting on the superiority of French gender relations, indeed, of associating them with higher forms of civilization. Although I do not want to reproduce that anxiety (rather I want to analyze it), I have found it impossible to make a rigorous or consistent distinction in my own terminology. My using "veil" and "headscarf" interchangeably reflects the way in which the words were deployed in the debates.

A similar set of conflations came with the word Muslim, a religious identification often (though not always) signified for women by the veil. Although it designated followers of the religion of Islam, "Muslim" was also used to refer to all immigrants of North African origin, whatever their religion. Sociologist Riva Kastoryano tells us that since at least the 1980s "immigrant," in France, has been synonymous with North African. Moreover, little distinction is made between North Africans, Arabs, and Muslims, although not all North Africans are Arabs, not all Arabs are Muslims, and not all Muslims in France come from North Africa. In the political discourse of French republicans, however, the different meanings are hard to distinguish, the terms bleed one into another. As with "veil," "Muslim" evokes associations of both inferiority and menace that go beyond the objective definition of the word itself: "Muslims" are "immigrants," foreigners who will not give up the signs of their culture and/or religion. Invariably, too, the religion they are said to espouse is painted as "fundamentalist," with incontestable claims not only on individual comportment but on the organization of the state. In this discourse the veil denotes both a religious group and a much larger population, a whole "culture" at odds with French norms and values. The symbolism of the veil reduces differences of ethnicity, geographic origin, and religion to a singular entity, a "culture," that stands in opposition to another singular entity, republican France.

For a small piece of cloth, the veil is heavy with meanings for French republicans who are worried about schools and immigrants, freedom and terrorism. Having an opinion about it serves to establish one's credentials on the heady topics of individualism, secularism, and the emancipation of women—it is an ideological litmus test. Banning the veil also became a substitute solution for a host of pressing economic and social issues; the law on headscarves seemed as if it could wipe away the challenges of integration posed for policymakers by former colonial subjects (most often perceived as poor and beyond redemption even if some were established members of the middle class). In a fascinating way, the veil in republican discourse served to cover a body of intractable domestic issues even as it revealed the anxieties associated with them. Getting beyond *that* veiling is the purpose of this book.

The answer to the question "why the veil?" then is complicated. Or perhaps a better word is "overdetermined." There were many reasons why French policymakers focused on the veil, even as they emphasized just one (the protection of women's equality from Islamist patriarchs). These reasons went beyond defending modernity against traditionalism, or secularism against the inroads of religion, or republicanism against terrorists. In this book I explore these reasons by treating separately the topics of racism, secularism, individualism, and sexuality, although all four were actually intertwined. To make sense of the complex fabric of French republican discourse on the veil, though, I have had to separate its interwoven strands. Each strand contributed to drawing and fortifying a boundary around an imagined France, one whose reality was secured by excluding dangerous others from the nation. At the same time, the political discourse of embattled republicanism created a firmer community of identification for Muslims than might otherwise have existed. The veil became a rallying point—something to defend as a common value—even for those who did not wear it.

My insistence on history and complexity is not just a scholarly indulgence; it has urgent political implications. Simple oppositions not only blind us to the realities of the lives and beliefs of others but create alternative realities that affect our own self-understanding. A worldview organized in terms of good versus evil, civilized versus backward, morally upright versus ideologically compromised, us versus them, is one we inhabit at our risk. It leaves no room for self-criticism, no way to think about change, no way to open ourselves to others. By refusing to accept and respect the difference of these others we turn them into enemies, producing that which we most feared about them in the first place. This has happened in France and, with local variation, elsewhere in the West. Indeed, the French law seems to have inspired other countries to follow suit in what is fast becoming a consolidation of sides in a clash between "Islam" and "the West." The inability to separate the political radicalism based in the religion of a few from the religious and/or customary practices, or simply the ethnic difference, of the many has alienated disaporic Muslim populations, even those who want nothing more than to become full citizens of the lands in which they live. And it has occured "us" in an inflexible and thus dangerously defensive posture in relation to "them."

I have not used the word toleration to talk about how we should deal with those radically different from ourselves because, following political theorist Wendy Brown, I think toleration implies distaste (her word is aversion) for those who are tolerated.[8] I want to insist instead that we need to acknowledge difference in ways that call into question the certainty and superiority of our own views. Instead of assimilation we need to think about the negotiation of difference: how can individuals and groups with different interests live together? Is it possible to think about difference non-hierarchically? On what common ground can differences be negotiated? Perhaps it is the common ground of shared difference, as French philosopher

Jean-Luc Nancy has suggested. Nancy argues that it is wrong to think of community as a shared essence, a common being, because that "is in effect the closure of the political." Instead, he says, we must recognize that we all share "being-in-common," which "has nothing to do with communion, with fusion into a body, into a unique and ultimate identity."⁹ Common being presupposes sameness while "being-in-common" says only that we all exist and that our very existence is defined by our difference from others. Paradoxically, it's difference that is common to us all.

We must stop acting as if historically established communities were eternal essences. This is one of the challenges of our time—one that French leaders were unwilling and unable to meet. Their story is for me an object lesson in politics, an example of the misuse of history and the blinding effects of hysteria. We need to think about the limits of their approach in order to develop alternatives to it—alternatives that will, of course, vary according to national context, but that will in each case allow for the recognition and negotiation of difference in ways that realize the promises of democracy.

1

THE HEADSCARF CONTROVERSIES

In France, debate about whether girls could wear Islamic head-scarves in public schools erupted at three separate moments: in 1989, 1994, and 2003. The chronological sequence does not reflect a steady increase in the number of headscarf-wearing girls or in acts by them which might be called disruptive. The girls were usually good students, with no disciplinary records. The only objection to them was that they insisted on wearing the hijab—the piece of cloth that became (as we shall see in what follows) a symbol of the "problem of Islam" for the French republic. What the chronological sequence does reflect is a hardening of the government's position in reaction to the steadily growing political influence of the anti-immigrant far right. From an early official inclination to tolerate expressions of individual religious conviction, there emerged a consensus that headscarves were dangerously political in their challenge to the principles of the secular republic and in their necessary association with Islamism and terrorism.

1989

The events that became known as the *affaires des foulards* began on October 3, 1989, when three Muslim girls who refused to remove their headscarves were expelled from their middle school in the town of Creil, about thirty miles outside of Paris. The school is in a "priority educational zone" (ZEP), one that is poor and ethnically mixed, with a high turnover in the teaching staff and a great deal of class, religious, and cultural tension. The principal, Ernest Chenière, once referred to it as "une poubelle sociale" (a social garbage pail). When he expelled the girls, he claimed to be acting to enforce "laïcité"—the French version of secularism. According to Chenière, laïcité—a concept whose meaning would be furiously debated in the months and years that followed—was an inviolable and transparent principle, one of the pillars of republican universalism. The school was the cradle of laïcité, the place where the values of the French republic were nurtured and inculcated. It was, therefore, in the public schools that France had to hold the line against what Chenière later termed "the insidious jihad."[1]

What would at other times have been a minor incident—a school principal disciplining a few of his students—quickly became a major media event, tapping into, and at the same time inflaming, public uneasiness about the place of North African immigrants and their children in French society. Although many of these "immigrants" had long lived in France—indeed, some had even been born there and were citizens—they were seen as strangers to the dominant culture. They were, for the most part, poor; they lived in suburban enclaves on the outskirts of major cities; and many were Muslims. At a moment of international attention to Islam and to Arab militancy—as exemplified in the Iranian ayatollah Khomeini's *fatwa* against Salman Rushdie and the start of the first Palestinian *intifada* against the Israeli occupation—as well as of national concern about the emergence in France of a few small militant Islamist groups, the anxiety about Islam in France (said now to be its second largest religion) was intense. Press coverage of the expulsion of the three girls, and then of other conflicts about headscarves in other schools with similar populations, served to focus that anxiety, making a few schoolgirls' choice of attire the symbol of a challenge to the very existence of the republic.

On the face of it, the hubbub generated by the press seems exaggerated, but in fact it exposed the crisis the nation was confronting: how to reconcile an increasingly multicultural population with a universalism that precluded the recognition of cultural and social differences. The celebrations of the bicentennial of the French Revolution in 1989 insisted that universalism was a defining and enduring trait of republicanism, the key to national unity. In many op ed pieces, commentators warned that tolerating displays of Islamic affiliation would lead France down the disastrous path of American multiculturalism: ethnic conflict, affirmative action which put race above merit, social fragmentation, and political correctness. The distorted depictions of the American experience offered a warning that France must resist all efforts to address the realities of its social and cultural pluralism.

In the press accounts, the Muslim hijab referred to in French as a headscarf (foulard) quickly became the veil (voile), or more dramatically, the chador, this last evoking the specter of an Iranian-style Islamic revolution. Predictably, perhaps, Catholic leaders (as well as Protestant and Jewish) joined some of their Muslim counterparts in decrying the expulsions, arguing that laïcité meant respect for and toleration of differences of religious expression among students. Less predictable was the split between the two leading antidiscrimination groups: one condoned, the other deplored, the expulsions, both in the name of the secular principles of the republic.[2] Demonstrations organized by Islamists to support the girls from Creil exacerbated the controversy; pictures of veiled women marching to protect their "liberty" and their "honor" only reinforced the idea of revolutionary Islam on the rise. The voices of calm and reason—those pointing out, for example, that radical, politicized Islam could be attributed to only a tiny minority of French Muslims, or that the number of headscarves in schools was hardly a widespread phenomenon—were drowned out by a growing hysteria fed by the pronouncements of some leading intellectuals. In an article published in the left-leaning magazine *Le Nouvel Observateur*, five philosophers ominously warned that "only the future will tell if the year of the bicentennial will also have been the Munich of the republican school."[3] The apocalyptic tone of their manifesto was, given the reality of the events, astonishing: "The foundation of the Republic is the school," they insisted, "that is why the destruction of the school will lead to the fall of the Republic." From this adamantly republicanist perspective there could be no accommodation with Islam.

Initially, however, there was accommodation. Overriding criticism from within and outside his party, Socialist minister of education Lionel Jospin managed to contain the situation by referring the matter to the Conseil d'Etat—the highest administrative court in France, whose task is to deal with the legality of actions taken by public bodies. On November 27, the council ruled that the wearing of signs of religious affiliation by students in public schools was not necessarily incompatible with the principle of laïcité, as long as these signs were not ostentatious or polemical, and as long as they didn't constitute "acts of pressure, provocation, proselytism or propaganda" that interfered with the liberties of other students.[4] Students could not be refused admission to school for simply wearing headscarves; this would be a violation of the right to individual conscience, which included religious conviction. Their behavior (putting pressure on other students to wear headscarves, refusing to participate in athletic activities or to attend classes that conflicted with their religious beliefs) also had to clearly challenge or disrupt public order before it could be legitimately restrained. Those best able to interpret this behavior, the council concluded, were the teachers and school administrators, who knew their pupils. In a ministerial circular based on the council's ruling, Jospin left it to local school authorities to decide, on a case by case basis, whether headscarves were admissible or not.

Despite some condemnations, the ruling did in fact calm things down, and media attention moved elsewhere. There was hardly any coverage of various local negotiations, except for the conclusion of the story of the girls from Creil. Two of the three (sisters of Moroccan origin) were convinced by the King of Morocco, whose intervention had been sought by some French Muslim leaders, to take off their headscarves when they entered a classroom. It is interesting to note in this connection that the pressure that was brought to bear from their "community" forced the girls to abandon their choice of religious expression in favor of accommodation to secular authority. The compromise—and indeed it was a compromise—didn't actu-

ally remove headscarves from schools; it just bared the heads of
the girls for the duration of each class. In a clear demonstration
of their personal religious conviction, they continued to wear
the hijab in the school's hallways and courtyards. But upon entering a classroom they were required, repeatedly, to enact def-
erence to the secular rules that their deportment and dress refused. The compromise, in other words, did not resolve but
rather made manifest the tension between France and its Muslim citizens. I do not qualify the term Muslim, despite the fact
that as many as 45 percent of Muslims polled at the time
agreed that the hijab should not be worn in school. Those republicans who wanted headscarves banned made no distinction between one Muslim and another. For them the headscarf
was a symbol, not only of those who defined themselves as orthodox followers of Islam, but of the entire Arab/North
African/Muslim population in France.

1994

In 1994, Ernest Chenière again raised the question of headscarves in schools. Now he was a deputy representing the de-
partment of the Oise for the center right party, the Raillement
pour la République (RPR). Elected to office as part of the
sweeping triumph of the right in the legislative elections of
1993, Chenière immediately offered a bill that would ban all
"ostentatious" signs of religious affiliation. After a year of what
one news account referred to as "Chenière's crusade," during
which there were several conflicts in schools (among them a
strike by teachers at one school in support of a gym instructor
who claimed that headscarves were dangerous to wear during

physical activity), the minister of education, François Bayrou, decreed on September 20, 1994, that "ostentatious" signs of religious affiliation would henceforth be prohibited in all schools.[5] The behavior of the students need not be taken into account, he asserted, because certain signs were "in themselves" transparent acts of proselytizing. Bayrou drew a distinction between "discreet signs," those that demonstrated personal religious conviction, and "ostentatious signs," whose effect was to introduce difference and discrimination into an educational community that, like the nation it served, ought to be united. Indeed, the nation was the only community which could command the allegiance of its citizens. "The nation is not simply a collection of citizens with individual rights. It is a community."[6] Discreet signs were tolerable; ostentatious signs were not.[7] The ministerial pronouncement was followed by the expulsion of sixty-nine girls wearing what were increasingly referred to as "veils."

As in 1989, there was a huge media controversy, and many of the same arguments were rehearsed.[8] As earlier, the situation was likened to the Dreyfus Affair, the dispute over what turned out to be a spurious charge of treason brought against a Jewish army captain at the end of the nineteenth century. Each side was adamant. Those supporting Bayrou came from across the political spectrum; their tone was urgent. They inevitably linked events in France to the violent civil war then raging in Algeria. A principled defense of the republic required decisive action, they insisted. One could not tolerate the expression of a religiosity that was itself inherently intolerant and oppressive. Those opposing the minister's decree included a handful of academics and (again) representatives of France's religious establishment. Sociologists Françoise Gaspard and Farhad Khos-rokhavar interviewed girls who wore the hijab in an effort to demonstrate the complexity and diversity of their motives. "If one accepts the postulate that the royal road to liberation is through education," they wrote, "then to reject girls with veils . . . is to penalize them . . . by denying them the possibility of becoming modern."[9] Although Gaspard and Khosrokhavar were often attacked as proponents of the veil, in fact their argument accepted the same opposition between tradition and modernity, religion and enlightenment used by those who favored expulsion of veil-wearing students. The difference was more than tactical, however. Bayrou and his followers were engaging in symbolic politics (France takes a stand against Islam), while Gaspard and Khosrokhavar were interested in practical outcomes: they believed that negotiation, not exclusion, would lead to the desired end of integrating Muslims into French society as well as promote feminist goals of education and emancipation.

Bayrou's decree was challenged by some of the girls who had been expelled from school, and it was overturned by various courts and by the Council of State, which reaffirmed its 1989 ruling. The council rejected Bayrou's claim that certain signs could be separated from the intentions of those who carried them and again left it to teachers and administrators to interpret the actions of their students. In the wake of this ruling, Simone Veil, the minister of social affairs, appointed a woman of North African origin, Hanifa Chérifi, as official mediator for problems linked to the wearing of the veil. Chérifi's work seems to have borne fruit: the number of disputes dropped dramatically (from about 2,400 in 1994 to 1,000 in 1996), and only around a hundred students were reported to be wearing headscarves to class. In some schools, girls were permitted to wear bandanas to cover their hair (although there were often intricate negotiations about size and color); in others, headscarves could be worn in the school building as long as they were dropped to the shoulders upon entering a classroom. As in 1989, the compromises did not resolve the tension but embodied it.

The controversy again died down, although it continued to receive government attention, in no small part because of insistent pressure from the increasingly visible, far-right populist party, the National Front. In 2000, the High Council on Integration, a body appointed by the government to address issues of immigration, made a number of recommendations about how to deal with "Islam in the Republic." In what political scientist Marc Howard Ross calls a "soft" republican approach, and what seems to me to be an exercise in equivocation, the report recognized the difficulty of excluding students with headscarves at the same time that it defined the wearing of these as antithetical to the goal of "integration."[10] It endorsed efforts at mediation rather than the passage of laws. But it did not resolve the ongoing tension between the definition of France as a nation "one and indivisible," in which difference was rendered invisible, and the increasing social and cultural diversity of its population.

2003

In 2003, the question of headscarves was first brought to national attention when the minister of the interior, Nicolas

Sarkozy, insisted that Muslim women pose bare-headed for official identity photographs. (Concern about terrorism after the attacks of September 11 in the U.S. was one of the justifications for this ruling.) In the wake of the controversy generated by the policy, schools once again became an issue, and politicians from the major parties rushed to declare their fealty to the republic. Socialist deputy Jack Lang presented a bill to the National Assembly that, in the name of laïcité (and in the interests of not being perceived as discriminating against Muslims), would outlaw signs of any religious affiliation in public schools. In June the assembly created an investigative body to gather information, and in July President Jacques Chirac appointed a commission headed by a former government minister and deputy, Bernard Stasi, to explore the feasibility of enacting a law.[11]

While the Stasi commission was meeting, press attention turned, at the end of September 2003, to two sisters in the suburban town of Aubervilliers (just outside of Paris). Alma and Lila Lévy were expelled from their high school when they refused either to remove their headscarves or to accept in its place a head covering the school administrators called "un foulard léger" (a headscarf "lite"!), which revealed the neck, earlobes, and hairline. (I will return to the question of what is covered and what is exposed in chapter 5). The girls had recently converted to Islam, much to the consternation of their parents and paternal grandmother, all of them leftists and avowedly secular. The father, a lawyer, referred to himself as "a Jew without God"; the mother, a teacher, was ethnically a Kabyle (a Berber, not an Arab) from Algeria who had been baptized as a Catholic but who did not practice her religion.

The parents were separated, one of the reasons for the girls' dismaying decision to convert, according to their grandmother. "It's not their fault. They are victims; they don't know how to find stability in a society that is too difficult for them," she wrote in *Le Monde*.[12] But she, like their father, insisted on the girls' right to attend school in whatever costume they chose: "I detest their conversion, their veil, their headscarf and their prayers to Allah, but I love them and want them to be happy and I believe that it is only through the education they receive in the course of their studies that they will be able, perhaps, to no longer need Islam, which for the moment is necessary to them."[13] "I'm not in favor of the headscarf," the father commented, "but I defend the right of my children to go to school. In the course of this business I've discovered the hysterical madness of certain ayatollahs of secularism who have lost all their common sense."[14]

The Lévy case was particularly interesting because there was no family pressure to wear the hijab, nor did the girls belong to any Islamic group. (The conversion of these girls may have made the case especially worrisome, since it demonstrated that Islam had the power to supplant even a secular upbringing.) One other girl, from a North African family, initially joined the two sisters but later had to relinquish her struggle, she told reporters, because her father beat her for wearing a headscarf. In all three instances, the decision seems to have been an individual one, contrary to the explanations offered by those who sought to ban the foulard in order to liberate women from the control of Islamist men. The Lévy sisters had only occasionally been to a mosque, yet they followed what they took to be the precepts of their chosen faith. They prayed five times a day,

fasted during Ramadan, studied the Koran, began to learn
Arabic, and listened to tapes of some leading theologians,
among them Tariq Ramadan, the Swiss Muslim scholar. They
wore a long veil over their clothing (removing it when they got
to school) and a headscarf (tucked into a turtle-neck shirt), in
order to attain the modesty they thought their religion required of them.[15] Theirs were individual decisions, which while
religious might well be read also as exquisite gestures of adolescent rebellion, or as attempts to challenge mainstream society
as the girls' parents had, though in a completely different id-
iom from the left-wing politics of the older generation (a politics no longer available in a postcommunist age). Indeed, one
sociologist, commenting on the headscarf controversies, suggested that for young dissidents in the twenty-first century,
identifying with Islam was the functional equivalent of the
Maoism of the 1960s and 70s. There was as little room, however, for an examination of motives in this case as in any of the
earlier headscarf controversies. The issue was debated less in
terms of the individuals involved than in terms of the symbolic
positions attributed to them.

As in 1989 and 1994, debate was intense. But now that a
commission was considering recommending a law, the stakes
were higher. Those on the left in favor of a law excluding headscarves from schools likened those they called Islamic fundamentalists to Nazis and warned of the danger of totalitarianism
(Iran was a favorite example). Those on the left opposed to exclusion saw the law as a continuation of French colonial policy:
Arabs were still being denied rights of self-determination by a
racist republic. *Their* critics, in turn, accused them of naive leftism. Among leftists, as among feminists, the question of the

status of women in Islam was also at issue. Those who favored a law banning headscarves (including some women from countries with oppressive Islamic regimes) saw it as a blow for women's emancipation, a sign that France would not tolerate oppressive, patriarchal practices. The far-left party Lutte ouvrière, for example, supported interdiction of the veil as a way of refusing "the infamous oppression of women."[16] And the editors of the feminist journal *ProChoix* attacked those who urged tolerance as being guilty of dangerous "cultural relativism."[17] Those who opposed a law, in contrast, insisted that the expulsion of girls with headscarves would not emancipate them but drive them either to religious schools or into early marriages, losing forever the possibility of a different future. If these girls were victims of manipulation, then barring them from school amounted simply to punishing the victim. How could that be called emancipation?[18] Others warned against treating girls with headscarves as victims. "We want to consider veiled girls or prostitutes as subjects, not victims. So we must listen to what they have to say," cautioned a representative of Femmes publiques (Public Women), an advocacy group for prostitutes. But in the dozens of articles and books published in 2003, it was rare to find the voices of the girls whose fate was at issue. Until a book of interviews with them was published in 2004, even the Lévy girls—who were at the center of the controversy—had little chance to explain themselves.

As the pages of newspapers and journals filled with debate, as friends and families stopped talking about the issue because it so bitterly divided them, the Stasi commission held interviews and long meetings. It issued its report, "Laïcité et République," in December. The report reaffirmed the hallowed traditions of secularism, and on these grounds called for the outlawing of all "conspicuous" signs of religious affiliation in public schools. Its recommendations also included recognition of a need to tolerate varieties of religious practices and even to adopt policies that were more inclusive than in the past. Acknowledging the reality of the pluralistic nature of French society, the commission called for "full respect for spiritual diversity"; the addition of instruction in the history and philosophy of religions to the educational curriculum; the establishment of a national school for Islamic studies; the creation of Muslim chaplaincies in hospitals and prisons; alternatives to pork for Muslims and Jews in school, prison, and hospital cafeterias; and the recognition of Yom Kippur and Aïd-El-Kébir as national holidays.

Despite all kinds of significant qualifications (for example, that the acceptance of the country's spiritual diversity must not be allowed to diminish the historic place of Christianity in French culture, which meant that religious teaching continued in state schools in the Alsace-Moselle region), these recommendations granted the need to adopt policies that ended the marginalization of Muslims and that would make them feel more fully a part of French society. They were meant to deny the charge that the headscarf ban was a rejection of Muslims in general. For a few members of the commission these recommendations were as important as the headscarf ban, because they signaled that the law did not apply solely to Muslims, that it was not discriminatory in intent. But—in a sign of what could only be read as a hardening of the government position—the sole recommendation accepted by Chirac in January 2004 was for a law prohibiting the wearing of conspicuous signs of religious affiliation in public schools. Yarmulkes and Sikh turbans were also swept away by this law which, despite that, was popularly referred to as the headscarf law. There was to be no room for the compromises that had been negotiated in years past (scarves on shoulders, "lite" scarves, bandanas); the law was designed to dispel the tensions these compromises had embodied. It became the law of the land in March 2004, and its enforcement began the following October. Without the softening effect of the other recommendations, the head scarf ban became a definitive pronouncement: there would no longer be compromises or mediation—it was either Islam or the republic.

Timing

There are many explanations to be offered for the hardening of the government position. The years between 1989 and 2003 saw a dramatic increase in international attention to political Islam, even if it did not see an increase in the number of head-scarf conflicts in French public schools. Events in Iran, Israel/Palestine, Algeria, New York City, Afghanistan, and Iraq certainly contributed to anxiety about the place of Muslims in France, despite the fact that polls continued to show that the vast majority of Muslims were becoming more secular, more integrated into French society. There was, to be sure, a more visible and outspoken Islamist presence in France in 2003 than there was in 1989 (though its numbers were still small), and there were more "hot spots"—schools in which young male militants were seeking ways to challenge secular values and practices. But putting pressure on girls to wear headscarves was

among the more benign of activities which included wearing
distinctive clothing and beards, as well as refusing to attend
history or gym classes that were at odds with their beliefs and
practices. It is hard to conclude, then, that the decision to pass
a law banning headscarves from public schools was a reaction
to an objective worsening of these circumstances. Rather we
must look both to domestic politics and to the international
climate (migrations of former colonial subjects, global economic pressures, transnational diplomatic events) to explain
the timing of the *affaires* and the decision to pass a law banning headscarves in 2004.

The intensifying determination of successive governments
to address the Muslim question—symbolically, by taking a firm
stand on headscarves—came in reaction to the growing popularity and electoral success of Jean-Marie Le Pen's populist
National Front party. The *affaires des foulards* are episodes in
the continuing drama of Le Pen's challenge to the mainstream
parties, and the timing almost exactly coincides. Le Pen managed, during the 1980s and 90s, to build a formidable machine
by focusing on the issue of immigration. When he refers to
"immigrants," he means those of North or West African origin, who may or may not be Muslims and who are often sec-
ond- and third-generation French, so not immigrants at all.
But Le Pen defines them all as immigrants to emphasize their
foreignness.

Beginning in 1983, Le Pen entered the electoral field, and
his party slowly gained footholds in a few municipal and regional councils. In the presidential election of 1988 the tide
turned for him. Much to his satisfaction, Le Pen created a
panic when he won 14 percent of the vote in the first round.

The next year, the National Front had a strong showing in elections for the European parliament. In the elections for the European parliament in 1994, the National Front scored even better, gaining eleven seats. In the first round of the presidential election of 2002, Le Pen came in second. In reaction, there were huge demonstrations in Paris and elsewhere in defense of the republic, and in the second round of the election, his opponent, Jacques Chirac, the leader of a coalition of parties of the right, won by a landslide. But even with this decisive defeat, Le Pen is perceived as a continuing threat to the established parties, as well as to the republic they claim to represent. The conservatives keep looking for ways to recapture the constituencies they have lost to him (although they are not above allying with the National Front in order to defeat Socialist Party candidates), and the left also worries (rightly) that the immigration issue has stolen increasing numbers of its working-class votes. Le Pen's role—pushing parties of the right, left, and center to take firmer stands on "immigrants"—is characteristic of what's happening elsewhere in Europe. Laws regulating Muslims—sometimes spurred by a radical political attack in the name of Islam (the murder of Theo van Gogh in Holland, subway and bus bombings in London), sometimes offered simply as a substitute for costly social supports—come in response to populist or nationalist demands for action. The premise of these laws is that violent action is typical of Islam, and they at once foreclose other options for integration and consolidate diverse groups of Muslims into Roy's "virtual" communities.

Many French political leaders did not contest Le Pen's attribution of France's social problems to "immigrants" but offered different solutions. None of these proposals were very satisfactory because for the most part they were watered-down versions of Le Pen's: instead of expelling "immigrants" from France, expel girls with headscarves from French public schools, for example. In 1989 the expulsions at Creil followed Le Pen's strong showing in the presidential election the year before; Bayrou's ministerial circular and the sixty-nine expulsions in 1994 followed the National Front's winning seats in the European parliament; and Chirac's law came shortly after he defeated Le Pen in the second round of the presidential election of 2002. In each case, the fear of Le Pen's party pushed more moderate parties farther to the right.

A good illustration of this process is the path followed by Ernest Chenière, the principal of the school in Creil, instigator of the first *affaire* in 1989. As celebrations of the bicentennial became the occasion for repeated assertions of the sanctity of universalism and the dangers of "communalism," Chenière, a black man from the Antilles, decided to display his republican credentials and, it seems too, to set the stage for his political career. Already active in the RPR and one of those in the party who sought closer ties to the National Front, Chenière took a stand on "immigrants" by refusing to accept them in his school if they did not dress in conformity with secular standards. By 1994, he had won a seat in the assembly—presumably at least in part as a result of his outspoken stand against Islam—and from there he continued his demands for a clear policy on headscarves, pressing Bayrou to issue his decree. No concessions must ever be made to ethnic or religious difference, Chenière insisted. And if, unlike Le Pen, he was willing to admit "foreigners" to citizenship, it was only when—as individuals (like himself)—they embraced the values and identity of the French.

Another illustration comes from 2003, in the wake of Le Pen's presidential challenge. The parties of the right were in power, seeking at once to dispel the charges that the state discriminated against its Muslim population and to hold off criticisms from Le Pen that they were capitulating to Islamic extremism. Responding to claims that Islam was being treated differently from other religions (and that this unequal treatment was a source of disaffection and a spur to radicalism), the minister of the interior, Nicolas Sarkozy, created a national representative body for Muslims to parallel those of Catholics, Protestants, and Jews. These confessional councils deliberate on such matters as state support for religious schools, make recommendations about chaplains in hospitals and prisons, and offer opinions about what impact proposed laws will have on their constituencies. In a nation that is avowedly secular, the councils are a way of taking religion into account, and they are a means for the state to gain a measure of control over religious leaders—to create acceptable religiosities. The Conseil français du culte musulman (CFCM) came into being in April 2003. Elected by representatives of mosques and Islamic associations, it is now the official voice of French Muslims. The representatives are a mix of moderate and radical, but the strong showing of l'Union des organizations islamiques de France (UOIF), a radical group, confirmed the fears of those who thought that any Islam is, unlike Christianity or Judaism, antithetical to republicanism. And it had the worrisome potential to provide more grist for Le Pen's mill. The UOIF had been a particularly vocal advocate of the wearing of headscarves in public schools.

So the proposition by Socialist deputy Jack Lang in June and the quick action by the National Assembly (controlled by a coalition of parties of the right) and the president in July can be seen as a reaction to UOIF influence on the CFCM, a way of countering the official recognition of the UOIF as a voice for Muslims with an official prohibition of headscarves in schools. The state might have to recognize radicals when they were voted onto a representative religious body, but their influence would be curbed at the door of the school.

The strong stand taken against headscarves was, in fact, a sign of the impotence and/or unwillingness of the government to address the problem it shares with many other European nations: how to adjust national institutions and ideologies that assume or seek to produce homogeneity to the heterogeneity of their current populations. Capitulating to pressure from the far right only compounds the problem by accepting its Manichean terms and suggesting that resistance to change is the only possible solution. But it is precisely the Le Penist hysteria about "immigrants" that has made alternatives difficult to explore, by turning a disadvantaged and discriminated-against social group into a scourge and by conflating all Arabs with North Africans and all North Africans not only with Islam but with politically driven Islamism. The insistence that all Muslims are Islamists (and so terrorists or potential terrorists) distracts from the very real issues of social, economic, and religious discrimination faced by those of North African origin—issues that, in the absence of other solutions, Islamists have been able to exploit. Islam was taken to stand not only for religious difference but for a "culture" that caused the social marginality of these "immigrants." The effect of the affaires des foulards was to make the headscarf the symbol of a difference that could not be integrated.

Conclusion

It would be a mistake to blame the hostility to headscarves entirely on the influence of Jean-Marie Le Pen. While there is no doubt that the popularity of his anti-immigrant stance has forced the mainstream parties of the right and left to try to coopt his message, there is also no doubt that Le Pen taps into a set of racist attitudes with deep roots in French history. What some have referred to as "Islamophobia" antedates not only the attacks of September 11 and the war on terrorism but also the Algerian War. It is an aspect of the long history of French colonialism that began at least as early as the conquest of Algeria in 1830. In that history, the veil has played a significant part as a continuing sign of the irreducible difference between Islam and France—a difference (as I will argue in chapter 5) that gains force by its implicit reference to the irreducibility of the difference between the sexes. The veil, however, signifies not only religious incompatibilities but also ethnic/cultural ones. For that reason, we cannot understand the intense controversy generated by a few girls in headscarves without a consideration of the place of the veil in the history of French racism.

2

RACISM

My first encounter with French racism came in 1967, while I was doing research for my dissertation at the bureau of civil registry in the town of Carmaux, once a town of miners and glass-bottle blowers, in the southern central portion of France known as the Languedoc. It was a good place to get a sense of social dynamics; all kinds of people came into the office to register marriages, births, and deaths and to acquire identity papers. The men who staffed the office often chatted with natives of the region in the local patois (much to my confusion when I first got there), and they provided running commentary on the foreigners who came to record the vital events of their families' lives. While, once, these foreigners had come from other European countries (Spain especially) to work in the mines, now the immigrants were from the Maghreb, the region in North Africa consisting of the former French colony (Algeria) and protectorates (Morocco and Tunisia). Tensions were high in Carmaux and its environs. Though the Algerian War had ended in 1962, and with it nominal French control of a now independent Algeria, those who had opposed independence were still active. Indeed, on our Sunday family excursions we often confronted roadblocks as the police searched for commandos of the Organisation de l'armée secrète (OAS), a clandestine group consisting of former French military officials in Algeria, as well as activist settlers (*colons*) who were still fighting to restore Algeria to France. Many *pieds noirs* (settlers of European origin from Algeria) had also come to the area, and they were notably hostile to the Arabs in whose name they had been expelled from a place they still considered an integral part of France.

Day after day as I sat in the office turning the pages of old record books, I witnessed classic expressions of petty racism. An Arab man would come in to declare the birth of a son. As was (and still is) customary, the office workers would shake his hand, usually twice (when he arrived and departed). The interview was invariably polite and formal. But as soon as the man left, the comments would begin. The person who had shaken the Arab's hand would rush to wash his own, making a fuss about how dirty "those people" were. The office staff would ridicule the name of the child ("they're always called Nasser or Mohammed"), and they'd recount horror stories about the dysfunctional lives of these infidels. I usually listened quietly, until one day I was drawn into the conversation. This happened because of news from America. Riots were exploding in Newark and Detroit (and in over a hundred other smaller cities) that summer, and my hosts wanted to know how it was that such terrible racism existed where I came from. In France, they told me, no such prejudice existed; no such riots would ever occur.

Not exactly an uncritical American patriot (this was still the era of the war in Vietnam), I nonetheless objected. "But you have racism here too," I exclaimed. "Every day I listen to you saying terrible things about Arabs, the same terrible things white American racists say about blacks." "No, no," they replied, astonished at my ignorance, "our attitudes are not racist; they are based in fact. These people are animals, they are not Christians; your blacks are Christian. The Arabs don't live in real houses but in huts, in holes in the ground; they're uncivilized, uneducated, unclean. Listen to their music; watch how they dance; they have a natural [or was it unnatural?] rhythm all their own. Your blacks were once slaves; these Arabs have no such excuse. This is just how they are; this is the way the Koran teaches them to be." In this discourse, no distinction was made between Muslims and Arabs; if there were Arab Christians, they were not visible. Ethnicity and religion were taken to be a single package, each negatively reinforcing the other. Though Arabs were not referred to as a separate "race" (the word has largely disappeared from French vocabulary since the Holocaust), their status as "natives" (*indigènes*) amounted to the same thing in its insistence on their fundamental difference and inferiority.

After I recounted this experience to some friends who were schoolteachers in Albi, they invited me to speak to their classes about the similarities between French and American racism. When I talked to the students about how alike the negative attributions were, I was greeted with astonishment and the same kinds of objections I had encountered in the civil registry office. So firmly rooted were these attitudes, so much a matter of "common sense," that it was hard to grant credibility to an alternative point of view.

Although expressions of bias against Muslims must be viewed in their immediate contexts, they draw on a deep reservoir of racism that extends at least as far back as the early nineteenth century, the moment of the first conquest of Algeria in

1830. When I say racism, I refer to historian George Fredrickson's definition: "It is when differences that might otherwise be considered ethnocultural are regarded as innate, indelible, and unchangeable that a racist attitude or ideology can be said to exist."[1] He continues, "My theory or conception of racism . . . has two components: *difference* and *power*. It originates from a mind set that regards 'them' and 'us' in ways that are permanent and unbridgeable. . . . In all manifestations of racism . . . what is being denied is the possibility that the racializers and the racialized can coexist in the same society, except perhaps on the basis of domination and subordination."[2] Historically, French conceptions of Muslims fit this description: Muslims/Arabs have been marked as a lesser people, incapable of improvement and so impossible to assimilate to French ways of life. At various times, of course, different traits were singled out to represent Arab/Muslim inferiority; these could be religious or agricultural practices, presumed sexual proclivities, family organization, or articles of clothing such as the fez for men and the veil for women. My argument in this chapter is that we cannot understand contemporary debates about the veil without this history: in French eyes, the veil has long been a symbol of the irreducible difference and thus the inassimilability of Islam.

Colonial Legacies

When the French arrived in Algeria in 1830, they embarked on a campaign of military pacification that lasted until the 1870s; then they introduced civilian administration aimed at governing the territory that in 1848 had become three departments of France. From the outset, the violent imposition of

French rule was justified in terms of a "civilizing mission"—the bringing of republican, secular, universalist values to those who lacked them. Some of these values were Western, not specifically French, but the French considered their own version of them superior to all others and hence felt entitled to treat colonial subjects in a way that was different from other European empires: the colonizers aimed to assimilate these underdeveloped peoples to French culture. The notion of "mission" implied that assimilation was possible—one day Algerians, of whatever background, might become French. But on the other hand, and at the same time, the colonial adventure was legitimized by racist depictions of Arabs (Muslims, North Africans—the designations tended to overlap and merge) which inevitably called into question the very possibility of the civilizing project.

Islam in particular marked these people as a race apart. It was not simply a religion that, like French Catholicism, had to be tamed in the interests of science and reason, though there were surely some who drew that parallel. There was, for many of those who supported the imperial mission, something excessive about Islam. Alexis de Tocqueville, whom we revere as the author of *Democracy in America*, expressed this clearly in 1843: "I must say that I emerged convinced that there are in the entire world few religions with such morbid consequences as that of Mohammed. To me it is the primary cause of the now visible decadence of the Islamic world."[3] To be uplifted, then, these people had to be separated from their religion, but the project was not that easy because Islam was taken to be at once the cause *and* the effect of their inferiority. The logic ran this way: Muslims suffer from their religious beliefs, but these beliefs tell you something about the propensity of Arabs to decadence. Here was the paradox of the civilizing mission, and it persists to this day: the stated goal was to civilize (to assimilate) those who finally could not be civilized.

As the French settlers (colons) claimed some 675,000 hectares of farmland and 160,000 hectares of forestland in the first forty years of rule, they introduced massive changes in agriculture. The aim was to implant the French presence permanently, to displace indigenous populations and replace them with representatives of "civilization," not unlike the conquest of Native American lands by American settlers. Indeed, the American example was very much on the minds of statesmen such as François Guizot, in 1846 the minister of foreign affairs. In America, as in India, he reminded his audience, and now in Algeria, one is faced with "people who are half savages," accustomed to "devastation" and "murder," and therefore "one is obliged to employ more violent and sometimes harsher methods than those who command the soldiers are naturally inclined to use."[4] The French settlers shifted cultivation from wheat to wine, substituted private property rights for communal land ownership, and developed market economies in place of economies of exchange. In addition they waged what historian Edmund Burke III refers to as a *kulturkampf*, closing religious schools and libraries and seizing the properties of the Islamic foundations that supported them.[5] All of this to eliminate any basis for indigenous resistance to the imposition of French rule. It was Tocqueville who argued in 1846 that whole villages must be wiped out, their inhabitants not killed off but dispersed, if France were to conquer this territory and thus reestablish her preeminence as a European power.[6] "Once we have committed that great violence of conquest," he wrote,

"I believe we must not shrink from the smaller violences that are absolutely necessary to consolidate it."[7] By the early twentieth century, with conquest well completed, the process of domination in the name of superiority continued. Wrote one commentator in 1903, "Intellectually superior, morally superior, economically superior, the colon will drive out the Arab, only leaving him those lands which he [the colon] judges too poor to make use of."[8]

The inhabitants of Algeria were classified hierarchically by the French rulers. Algeria was deemed an integral part of France in 1848, but it was not until 1865 that a law defined as citizens settlers of French and European origin. In 1870, citizenship was extended to Algerian Jews, though Jews already were considered French nationals in the metropole. In the hierarchy of social distinction, Jews ranked below Christian Europeans and "native" French, but above the Muslims (Arab and Berber) who were the real subject peoples, those with no vote and no right to representation. Berbers, however, were deemed superior to Arabs because it was said that their belief in private property, their commerce and family law, as well as their European looks (blonde or red hair, blue eyes) made them more likely to assimilate to French ways. And, indeed, the greater tendency of Berbers to convert to Christianity was often taken as proof of this superiority. Above all, however, the fact that they were not Arabs was the key to Berber acceptability and the reason they were often selected to fill lower-level positions in the colonial administration. The conflict between France and Islam, enunciated at first in military terms—one French general called the followers of Islam "our eternal enemy"—and then in social and cultural terms, was evident in a law of 1919 that extended naturalization only to those Arab men who were willing to relinquish their "indigenous" status, which included following Islamic law.[9]

In their quest to maintain an empire, the French supplemented force with information. Because it was important to know one's subjects as well as to subdue them, scholars, administrators, and technicians produced studies of Arab culture and Islam. Some of this material was—from the natives' point of view—insightful and accurate, but much of it served to ratify the images of Arab difference and inferiority offered by colonial administrators and settler representatives. One study that became a model for later ethnographers purported to "tear off the veil which still hides the mores, customs, and ideas" of Arab society.[10] Many of the studies stressed the undercivilized nature of the Arabs. One, in 1903, described Algerians as of "limited intelligence and completely apathetic," given to the vices of "dissimulation and dishonesty, distrust and lack of foresight, love of sensuality, lechery and reveling."[11] More nuanced was the opinion offered by some scholars about the wisdom of trying to make Arab (Muslim) Algerians French. The colony, one of these commented in 1900, was "a piece of the East where race is so tenacious and traditions are so strongly resistant [to change] that groups of men cohabit there without ever losing their original character or amalgamating with one another."[12] He urged that French rule in Algeria follow the lines taken in the protectorate of Tunisia (acquired in 1881) rather than pursue the more difficult and probably impossible goal of eventual assimilation. But unlike the other North African territories (Morocco became a protectorate in 1912), Algeria *was* defined as an integral part of France itself. As a result, the contradictions between the civilizing rhetoric of French colonial policy and the racism that was at once its justification and its effect were played out with dramatic intensity.

Residents of France learned about North Africa from newspapers (often with illustrated lithographs), novels, and textbooks. For the most part these emphasized the exoticism of the "East," the profound differences between France and its "others." Even when the comments were meant to be benign, they conveyed French superiority and great condescension. For example, in 1913, French schoolchildren could read that "France wants little Arabs to be as educated as little French children. This shows how our France is bountiful and generous to the people she has conquered."[13] There were also travelers' accounts written from many perspectives and, at a more intimate level, postcards sent home by tourists vacationing in the exotic Maghreb. Although there was never unanimity about the French colonial project, there did emerge a consensus about the inferiority and/or strange customs and behaviors of North Africans: their cultural difference defied transformation.

In 1914, as war created a demand for manpower, especially in the armaments industry, a law granted Algerians, as members of the nation-state, the right to emigrate to France. (Moroccans and Tunisians did not have this right and so came to France illegally.) In the next fifteen years, increasing numbers of poor peasants, virtually all of them men, many of whom had lost their land to European settlers, arrived looking for jobs. (Their numbers swelled from 30,000 in 1914 to 130,000 in 1930, to 250,000 by 1950.) The presence of North Africans in the cities of the metropole, and the conditions under which they lived and worked, had the effect of exacerbating differences. Upon arrival by ferry in Marseille, the migrants were separated from the French passengers and treated roughly by police and customs agents. The jobs they found were of the worst sort: the work was dirty and unskilled, the pay minimal, and the social supports nonexistent. The men lived in cramped housing, clustered in neighborhoods that quickly were associated with high levels of prostitution, homosexuality, and crime. A report for the city of Paris on the conditions in which these migrants lived expressed appropriate horror at the situation of the men, but its tone and choice of words inevitably fed the perception that somehow they were less than human—only animals could tolerate such conditions: "In an area hardly larger than a hectare were makeshift shacks built with the debris from old huts and bits and pieces of rubbish, the whole often covered with tarred paper, and we stopped at the threshold paved with rubbish, requiring a strong stomach to confront the foul emanations. . . . And in these antechambers of every disease live, crowded as in a rabbit hutch, nearly a thousand men."[14]

Neil MacMaster shows, in his important book on colonial migrants, the ways in which during the 1920s a climate of racism was fueled by the colonial lobby, eager to keep cheap labor working in Algeria, and by French government officials, especially at the ministry of the interior, who worried about security in the nation's cities. French workers, too, were fearful of competition from the migrants; especially when war broke out in 1914, they assumed they would be sent to the front and that cheap North African labor would replace them at home. The hostility continued after the war, making it extremely difficult for trade unions or the Communist Party to organize migrants.

Despite their internationalist commitments, a report in 1926 concluded, French communists "in the factories . . . still have the widespread habit of considering the Arabs as inferior."[15]

Arabs in French cities were defined as criminals. One of the leading newspapers of the day, *Le Matin*, commented in 1923: "The crimes and offences committed by Arabs are increasing . . . almost all the rabble which infests us is foreign."[16] The crimes were most often depicted as sexual, a sign that Arabs lacked "civilization" and sometimes assumed to be a consequence of the low numbers of women in the migrant population. But the most frequent explanation had to do with innate Arab tendencies. In the hysteria surrounding the murder of two women by a mentally ill North African in 1923, rumors spread wildly and a crowd beat and killed an Arab man. "We are infested with Algerian natives," a neighbor complained, "dirty, ragged, working little, often drunk. They go down the street searching interiors with their eyes, insolent, looting, obscene. They inspire such fear that nobody dare complain or chase them away."[17] The image of the insolent, penetrating glare attached to Arabs as a group; they were "obscene," that is, excessively and unacceptably sexual. Prostitution was said to be rampant and homosexuality "almost normal" among Arab men, whose drives could not be otherwise satisfied. Describing the customs of North Africans in Paris, one observer noted in 1934 that "every week several workers . . . gather to recite litanies, to sing the mystical verses of Ibn al Fâridh or of Hallaj and to abandon themselves to ecstatic dances."[18] The ecstasy is so rapturous, so emotionally intense, that the dancer loses control of his reason and his senses. Here, in the image of the lascivious, dancing Arab man, is the racist stereotype. Given his perverse nature, it was best to keep one's distance and to contain him.

French policy did indeed insist on separation. In Paris, Muslims not only lived apart but were provided with separate hospitals. Until 1936, when a Muslim cemetery was built, they were buried in paupers' graves. In Lyon, rather than allow Muslims to remain buried with anonymous French paupers, their remains were removed in 1928. The administrator who ordered the removal declared (somewhat contradictorily, since there were no individual markings on these graves) that "they have been expunged from the sites of remembrance."[19]

In the face of discrimination and geographic segregation, Arabs in French cities tended to stick together. They undoubtedly found solace in the company of those with whom they shared language, religion, customs, kin ties at home, and a common experience of being foreign and despised on French soil. At the same time, there is evidence of migrant assimilation; some, for example, intermarried with French women, gave their children French first names, or wore European clothing. Adapting to French ways was in part an economic necessity, since labor often stipulated that workers dress in a certain way. The fez seems to have been retained for a longer time, on the streets and outside of work, gesturing to Muslim identity. But even when it had almost entirely disappeared among North Africans, French commentators refused to take the change as a sign of integration. "The fact that the fez is replaced by a cap evidently does not suffice to transform their character and values," concluded one writer.[20] So much for the possibilities of assimilation.

As migrants went back and forth from the metropole to

North Africa, settlers and colonial administrators worried that exposure to French society, and especially to leftist ideas of freedom and emancipation, would bring out the worst in them. The fear was less of assimilation—that didn't seem possible—than it was of awakened hopes and desires, the exposure to a different way of life without the restraining influences of tradition and religion. "These impulsive beings, with their violent desires, far from their habitual ways and religious leaders, are suddenly dominated by savage instincts," warned a colonial administrator.[21] This comment, of course, echoes the ones made in France about Arabs: the point was to restrain their savagery (by, among other things, tolerating religion and customary family law), whether in Paris or Algiers, or for that matter Rabat or Tunis. The interesting thing about the administrator's comment was that it conceded the futility of the "civilizing mission." It was tradition, not modernity, that would keep the Arab in his place.

Representations of Women

Although depictions of Arab men associated criminality and sex, it was Arab women who piqued the imagination of French colonialists, both in Algeria and in France. Early on, fantasies of conquest—the lure of wealth and exploration—were figured as sexual conquests. An archivist-historian has noted that the communications from combatants to their families were more fantastic than real: "The French army was . . . convinced that the taking of Algiers would open the route to the riches of the Orient. This impression, aided by imagination, was confirmed when . . . a Turk-Arab camp fell into our hands. On the cush-

ions piled in the chiefs' tents some convinced themselves they
saw the imprint of a woman's body. From then on, there was
not a military recruit who did not dream of treasures and con-
cubines."²² The "imprint of a woman's body" is one of those revealing "screen associations" which, as Freud has taught us,
substitutes one image (the female body in this case) for another
(imperial conquest). In this way the imperial project acquired
its deeply erotic overtones.

The subjugation of Algeria was often depicted by metaphors of disrobing, unveiling, and penetration. "The Arabs
elude us," complained General Bugeaud, the administrator of
the Algerian territory in the 1840s, "because they conceal their
women from our gaze."²³ Images of native women in novels of
the time stressed their volatility and the danger they posed.
"One senses feline claws beneath their caresses," wrote Thé-
ophile Gautier in 1845.²⁴ The pleasures and dangers of imperial domination and sexual domination were conflated in statements like these, and when marauding troops defeated native
resisters, it is not hard to see why they often celebrated their
victory by raping village women. Cartoons from the period il-
lustrate this theme: native women are carried off by victorious
French soldiers as "the spoils of victory." In the 1870s, there
were some administrators who, seeking to solidify French rule
and multiply their numbers, recommended—in a literalizing of
the conquest metaphors—that French men marry Arab
women. Argued one proponent of this strategy, "it is through
women that we can get hold of the soul of a people."²⁵ This
was also the aim of schools created for girls during the Third
Republic. Some were the work of feminists who wanted to
wean new generations of women from Arab culture and pro-

vide them the tools of emancipation (as it was defined in the West); others were the work of colonial administrators who sought to spare women from the humiliation they experienced in Arab households and win them over to French ways of life.

But more often it was as prostitutes that the colonists fantasized about Arab women. The Algerian writer Malek Alloula, reading postcards sold to tourists in the first three decades of the twentieth century, notes that the naked native women pictured on them are the "*very space of orgy:* the one that the soldier and the colonizer obsessively dream of establishing on the territory of the colony, transformed for the occasion into a bordello where the hetaeras are the women of the conquered."[26] The historian Marnia Lazreg recounts one way in which this dream transformed Algerian reality. In the first decades of their rule, the French encountered the Ouled Naïl people of the south. Although adherents to Islamic culture, women in this group had great sexual freedom and were renowned for their dancing. Unlike women from the north of the country, they did not wear veils. The colonists, however, took them to be prostitutes, embodiments of "the ancient Orient," and soon turned the area into a tourist attraction—what is today called a site of sexual tourism.[27] And the term "Ouled Naïl" became synonymous with "prostitute."

The numbers of prostitutes throughout the country increased as French settlers took over native farms, pushing peasants off the land, but the colonial rulers attributed to Islam and to Arab indolence the poverty that drove many women to sell sexual favors. Wrote one such administrator in 1850, "there exists a large number of girls who indulge in prostitution in all classes of the population. This is one of the saddest conse-

quences of . . . extreme poverty. . . . Such poverty is caused by
some vices inherent in Islamic law, and the great ease with
which . . . [Muslim judges] allow repudiation. For women who
are essentially ignorant, lazy, and unskilled, there is no other
means of subsistence than prostitution once their husbands
have repudiated them."[28] The governor-general of Algeria
added, in 1898, that these women were driven by their innate
sexuality; like their male counterparts, they were taken to be
embodiments of licentiousness. "The Arab man's, the native
Jew's and the Arab woman's physiology, as well as tolerance of
pederasty, and typically oriental ways of procreating and relating to one another are so different from the European man's
that it is necessary to take appropriate measures."[29] (He recommended segregating prostitutes by race.) Writing in 1900,
from another perspective, in a book meant to sympathetically
publicize the plight of women in this region, feminist Huber
tine Auclert confirmed some of these images in *The Arab
Women of Algeria*. She described the *casbah*, the old section of
the city of Algiers, in orientalist terms, as a place of unfettered
sexuality (not entirely a bad thing in her fantasy). There
women "stretched out on pillows, adorned and covered with
jewels, offer themselves, like madonnas on an altar, for the ad-
miration of passersby. . . . [I]t is not rare to see couples smile at
one another, embrace, entwine and tumble to the pavement . . .
abandoned to the transports of love."[30]

This public indulgence in sex was the opposite of the practice of sequestering women in the harem, which also fascinated
French observers. Even more than the veil, or perhaps as an ex-
tension of it, the harem—an all-female space to which men
could not be admitted—represented frustration of the coloniz-

ers' desire. Malek Alloula points out that the postcards he col-
lected—scenes staged in a photographer's studio and produced
for the tourist market, not real-life snapshots—document
colonial fantasies precisely because they are staged. In them the
harem is depicted as a jail; women are imprisoned behind bars,
inaccessible to the (white) men who lusted after them. "If the
women are inaccessible to sight (that is, veiled), it is because
they are imprisoned. This dramatized equivalence between the
veiling and the imprisonment is necessary for the construction
of an *imaginary scenario* that results in the dissolution of the
actual society, the one that causes the frustration, in favor of a
phantasm: that of the harem."[31]

The harem was imagined both as a place of sensuous indulgence and as a cage in which women were confined by tyranni-
cal men. There were those who equated Arab women with
prostitutes and those who envisioned them as slaves to their
husbands and families. Auclert referred to "cloistered women"
and to "women buried alive, whose husbands can strangle
them with impunity."[32] In either case, the reference was to all
women, suggesting the homogeneity of Arab females—they
were a type, and they were stereotyped. The historian Julia
Clancy-Smith argues that either as prostitutes or as abjected
servants, these women were taken to be the opposite of French
or settler women, thereby establishing the agency of the
French and the passivity of the Algerians as well as the nor-
malcy of European lives in juxtaposition to the perversity of
the Arabs. She cites a book (written in 1871 and published in
1912) by a General Melchior-Joseph-Eugène Daumas that
well illustrates this attitude. Daumas begins the book with a
request that is also a warning: "As the reader prepares to pene-

trate into the most intimate of matters in Muslim society, may his curiosity show indulgence for customs which can be revolting to European sensibilities."[33] Daumas was especially interested in sex and marriage and concluded that "the Arabs do not conceive of love in the same manner as we do."

Daumas's concerns repeated those of the Parisian public health official who argued in 1853 in favor of regulated prostitution for French forces in Algeria. Without it, he suggested, soldiers and settlers might be susceptible to the homosexuality that was "rampant" among natives because of the hot climate (in which "passions run higher") and the strict segregation of the sexes. When "young Algerian men are so handsome and go about in public unveiled, side by side with veiled females, homosexuality is thereby encouraged."[34] I will come back to this trope of the visible and the veiled in chapter 5; here I want simply to note another variation on the theme of perverse Arab sexuality, a theme that continued to preoccupy French writers well into the next century. Deprived of "normal" (that is, European-style) relations with women, it was believed that men became queer and the lines of sexual difference were bent and blurred. Auclert blamed native homosexuality on polygamy, which resulted, she said, in a shortage of wives. "Polygamy, which forces women condemned to endure it to resort regularly to the blade and to poison to get rid of a rival, leads men to pederasty."[35] She also objected to the customs of bride-price and child marriage. One of her chapters was called "Arab Marriage is Child Rape"; by implication all Arab marriages were rapes, even when the bride was of age.[36] Clancy-Smith cites a book by Professor Emile-Félix Gautier on Arab customs, written to celebrate the centennial of the conquest of Algeria. One of Gautier's conclusions attested to the impossibility of any commonality between Arab Muslims and the French: "Among the differences which oppose our Western society to Muslim society, if one searches to uncover that which is primordial, is the family."[37]

Kinship ties and family structures troubled Gautier and his predecessors less than the sexual practices they attributed to North African Muslims. Clancy-Smith suggests that the colonizers' writings about Arab women "demonstrated the immutable otherness of the indigenous population, especially when it came to matters of sexuality."[38] Here it is precisely the profusion of often contradictory images that testifies to the phantasmatic quality of the representations. In representations of Muslims, the strict separation of the sexes at once clarified and confused the rules of their interaction—not only within Muslim society, but between Muslims and French. The veil was a sexual provocation and a denial of sex, a come-on and a refusal. The harem was a prison and a brothel, a place of constraint and abandon. It enticed the putative conquerors and frustrated them; in the name of protecting female purity, the harem encouraged homosexuality in native men. Prostitution was a solution to Islam's rules about gender segregation and an effect of Islamic divorce law. And Islam itself, depicted as a cruel and irrational system of religious and social organization that must be replaced by enlightened French law, was also seen by some colonial spokesmen as necessary for keeping otherwise barbaric peoples under control. Islam was at once a symptom of innate Arab perversity and the cause of it, and this confusion of causality had the effect of stigmatizing both Arabs and Islam. It also laid bare the contradiction at the heart of the "civilizing mission," whose commitment to change and uplift could be confirmed only in juxtaposition to the permanent inferiority of those it claimed to be civilizing.

The Algerian War, 1954–1962

Nationalist movements of resistance to French rule in Algeria led to systematic warfare in 1954. In the bloody seven-year struggle that ensued, women became an object of attention for both sides, and the veil acquired tremendous political significance. In fact, it was at this time that the veil was first associated with dangerous militancy. It was not September 11, 2001, and the fear of Islamic terrorism that politicized the wearing of the veil; that had already happened during the Algerian War.

The National Liberation Front (FLN in French) declared its struggle to be a war of liberation from French rule. In response, the French in Algeria insisted that their presence was necessary for liberating Muslims from the grip of traditionalism. In France, those who increasingly saw the futility of holding on to this colony argued that Arabs could never be modernized, never assimilated. Thus Charles de Gaulle, who in 1962 would concede the war to the FLN, argued in 1959, in terms no less racist than his opponents, that Muslims could not be integrated into France because they would overwhelm it:

> We are, above all, a European people of the white race, of Greek and Latin culture and the Christian religion. . . . the Muslims, have you seen them . . . with their turbans and their djellabas? You can see clearly that they're not French! . . . Try to mix oil and vinegar. Shake the bottle. After a minute, they separate again. Arabs are Arabs,

French are French. Do you think that French society can absorb 10 million Muslims, who tomorrow will be 20 million and the day after that 40 million? If we integrate, if all the Arabs and Berbers of Algeria were to be considered French, how would we stop them from coming to the metropole, where the standard of living is so much higher? My village would no longer be Colombey-les-Deux-Eglises, but Colombey-les-Deux-Mosquées.[39]

Still, those who insisted that Algeria must continue to be French turned their attention to women, whom they encouraged to exchange their status as chattel for that of free citizens. Getting rid of the veil was a sign of this progress, evident in both the message and title of a film *(The Falling Veil)* made especially for American audiences by the French government. The film clearly influenced an article in the *New York Times* in July 1958 called "The Battle of the Veil." According to the author, the forces of modernity ("the French, the rebels, the Moslem youth of both sexes and even many older generation women") were pitted against the defenders of tradition, mostly elderly theologians. In fact, the battle was more complicated than that. If the veil had one symbolic meaning for defenders of French rule, it had several conflicting meanings for the resisters. It was, to be sure, a refusal of French appropriation of the country, a way of insisting on an independent identity for Algerians. But many of the leaders of the nationalist-socialist revolution also thought of themselves as modernizers. For them too the veil was a sign of backwardness that must eventually be overcome—but on Algerian, not French, terms. In addition, the veil became a useful instrument in the war against the French, permitting the clandestine transport of arms and bombs by militants of both sexes.

In response to the growing influence of the FLN, the French authorities in Algeria organized a network of "feminine solidarity" centers all over the country, dedicated to native women's emancipation. Sponsored by the wives of the occupation's military officers, the goal was to bring education to native women and so win their loyalty to the French cause. "Nourish the mind and the veil will wither by itself," said the wife of Brigadier General Jacques Massu, who led the movement in the capital city of Algiers. But to hasten this withering, the ladies joined a pro-France rally on May 16, 1958, at which they lifted the veils of their Muslim sisters—stripped them, as it were, of the protective cover of superstition and so exposed them to the "light." The women reportedly chanted happily, "Let's be like French women"—for the organizers of the rally, this was the voice of the indigene asking to be free.[40] The FLN at the time, and historians subsequently, have suggested that the chanting women were, in fact, so many humble villagers, impoverished women, perhaps also prostitutes and domestic servants, coerced into participating in a public relations event meant to show the world that the French were not colonizers but liberators and that the natives supported *L'Algérie française*. They add that the motive for removing the veil was also military: by 1958, the FLN was using veiled women to transport weapons and bombs past security checkpoints, so unveiling women was a way of depriving the rebels of a convenient disguise.

In the account of psychiatrist and FLN supporter Frantz Fanon, we can see that the status of the veil for the revolutionaries was a difficult issue. Although Fanon himself imagined a future in which traditional signs of inequality between women and men would disappear, he also understood the veil to be a way of resisting colonial domination. "It is the white man who creates the Negro. But it is the Negro who creates negritude. To the colonialist offensive against the veil, the colonized opposes the cult of the veil."[41] After May 16, he explained, it was particularly important to keep the veil: "In the beginning, the veil was a mechanism of resistance, but its value for the social group remained very strong. The veil was worn because tradition demanded a rigid separation of the sexes but also because the occupier *was bent on unveiling Algeria*."[42]

How to prevent this brutal appropriation and yet grant new agency to women was the dilemma of the revolutionaries, as Fanon recounts it. For him, the answer was to make women guerillas in the struggle on the same terms as men. "This is why we must watch the parallel progress of this man and this woman, of this couple that brings death to the enemy, life to the Revolution."[43] The challenge to Algerian women was both physical (the sheer danger of violent combat) and psychological: "She must consider the image of the occupier lodged somewhere in her mind and in her body, remodel it, initiate the essential work of eroding it, make it inessential, remove something of the shame that is attached to it, devalidate it."[44] In order to do this, the veil became not so much a sign of religious or cultural affiliation as it did an instrument of subversion. It was the means by which the abjection of colonial subjects could be transformed into a proud and independent national and personal identity.

After 1955, Fanon says, veiled women—at first the trusted

wives or widows of movement militants, later any willing women, some of whom had long since abandoned the veil— were used to transport messages, cash, and arms under cover. (In the 1966 film directed by Gillo Pontecorvo, *The Battle of Algiers*, men, too, use the veil to disguise themselves as women, in order to evade or sneak up on soldiers and military police.) When the army began to frisk women in veils, the women took another tack, dressing in European style (without veils) to gain access to parts of cities rarely frequented by Arabs, where they planted grenades or passed them to comrades who detonated them. Once the trick of the European look had been discovered by security forces, women militants returned to traditional dress. Comments Fanon, "Removed and reassumed again and again, the veil has been manipulated, transformed into a technique of camouflage, into a means of struggle."[45] The means (the veil) and the end (liberation) get permanently entwined in this moment, despite the FLN's critique of "traditionalism."

So potent an instrument did the veil become that French soldiers patrolling the countryside violated women first by forcibly removing their veils and then by raping them. Those suspected of being nationalists were treated even more harshly. Aahia Arif Hamdad told of her arrest along with her husband. As one soldier tore off her veil, another commented on its inauthenticity: "enough is enough; the game is over."[46] She was then beaten and subjected to electric shock as she stood nude, her veil replaced by a hood that prevented her from seeing her torturers. Although the hood was used in the torture of men as well as women, the symbolism in this case is important to note: one of the frequent complaints about the veil was that it allowed a woman to see without being seen. "This woman who sees without being seen frustrates the colonizer," wrote Fanon. "There is no reciprocity. She does not yield herself, does not give herself, does not offer herself. . . . The European faced with an Algerian woman wants to see."[47] In a clear act of revenge, the torture scenario reverses the situation: the hood blinds the woman while her interrogators get to look at her without limit. Yet another act of revenge came in the last days of the war, as de Gaulle was negotiating the Evian Accords in May 1962. The OAS abandoned its policy of shooting only men and fired on carefully chosen female targets as well: five veiled women (of whom three were killed) in the capital, Algiers.

The conclusion of the war could not resolve the multiple meanings of the veil. For the French, it continued to stand for the backwardness of Algeria, but it was also a sign of the frustration, even the humiliation, of France. It was the piece of cloth that represented the antithesis of the *tricolore*, and the failure of the civilizing mission. Immediately after the war, for the new leadership of the Algerian nation, the veil became a contested sign of the future direction of the country. The first president, Ben Bella, an internationalist and a socialist, urged women to shed the veil, explaining in 1963 that "it is not the wearing of a veil that makes us respect the woman, but the pure sentiments that we have in our hearts."[48] His successor, the more narrowly nationalist Colonel Boumedienne, who overturned Ben Bella in a military coup in 1965, warned Algerian women not to imitate their Western counterparts. "Our society," he said, "is Islamic and socialist," and he meant it in that order. The tension between a vision of a modern socialist nation, on the one hand, and a nationalist desire to restore Islamic and Arabic culture, on the other, was manifest in the different stands these leaders took on the question of the veil. There were also those who considered themselves progressive on social and economic issues but who nevertheless endorsed the veil as a legitimate expression of religious belief.

Suffice it to say here that the tension has continued in different forms to the present day, when a secular military government supported by France has managed for the moment at least to subdue a powerful challenge, which erupted into civil war in the 1990s, from Islamists (with external support from Saudi Arabia and elsewhere), among whose goals is veiling the women of Algeria. For these Islamists, however, as for the FLN in the 1950s, the veil is not simply a sign of the subjection of women (although it surely is that too). It also carries with it a sense of defiance, a refusal of the Western lifestyle and values of colonizers—whether classic imperialists or, now, global exploiters—and an insistence on the integrity of a history and religion that have for so long been demeaned. If for colonizers the veil was emblazoned with the stigma of ethnicity, for the colonized it became an antidote to domination. For a long time, much longer than the duration of the war of independence, the veil was—for colonized and colonizers alike—an impenetrable membrane, the final barrier to political subjugation.

The "Immigrant" Problem

Two million soldiers had fought to keep Algeria French; thirty-five thousand died in the process. The trauma of war continued long after the signing of the Evian Accords in 1962. OAS commandos roamed the French countryside, pursued by the police, and disaffected pieds noirs were mobilized by the far right in what would eventually emerge as a right-wing populist party, the National Front. The left cheered the liberation of the former colony, but watched with apprehension as the new Algerian nation took shape. Immediately after emancipation millions of migrants arrived in France, posing difficult questions (and leading to intricate rules) about what it meant to be French. This was the beginning of the marginalization of North African immigrants, who still occupy what sociologist Pierre Bourdieu referred to as a "liminal" status. "Neither citizen nor foreigner, nor really on the side of the Same, the 'immigrant' is found in this 'bastard' place of which Plato also spoke, the frontier between the social being and the social non-being."[49] It is precisely this liminal status—evidence of the continuing paradox of the civilizing mission—that was at issue in the headscarf controversies.

Under the Evian Accords, Algerians were granted special rights of access to the metropole, and children born to Algerian parents in France automatically became French citizens. Algerians were joined by Tunisians and Moroccans; together they represented the largest immigrant stream. In the early days, most migrants were men, a source of cheap and, many hoped, temporary labor, and they were encouraged to maintain ties with their home countries. In the 1970s, however, in part as a result of recommendations by the Council of Europe, families increasingly arrived together. Still anxious to think of this migration as temporary, the government provided social services to children in public schools—including Arabic language classes and religious instruction—thereby encouraging the differences that became grounds for discrimination. When the borders were closed in 1974, even those who had considered their stay temporary began to settle in large numbers. The expanded presence of the immigrant population, who lived in shanty towns (alongside poor French citizens) on the outskirts of major urban centers, combined with other events to bring renewed attention to the impact of North Africans. The stereotypes of colonialism were revived in debates about "immigrants," but the language of conquest was reversed. Now the question was whether the former colonial subjects would overrun the French homeland, whether, in particular, "Islam" would colonize "France." Muslims became an enemy within, neither entirely foreign nor yet fully members of the nation—an unassimilated, inassimilable presence that exposed the paradox of the civilizing mission and the ongoing failure of integration.

At first, attention focused on the economic impact of foreign workers, and they were often accused—by communists and trade unionists as well as populists—of displacing French workers. Indeed, during the economic slowdown of 1977–78, the conservative government of President Valéry Giscard d'Estaing encouraged North Africans to return home in order to open employment to more Frenchmen. There was controversy, too, during the 1970s about the sources of immigrant poverty: was it something in their "culture" that made them poor, or were they the victims of discrimination? The Iranian Revolution in 1978–79 changed the terms of these conversations, drawing attention away from economic and social influences to religion–to Islam as a dangerous presence on French soil.

The journalist Thomas Deltombe has tracked television coverage of immigrants and Islam between 1975 and 2005, and he shows clearly that the ascendancy of the Ayatollah

Khomeini in Iran ignited new concern about France's Muslim population. Although the Iranians were Shi'ites and the North Africans Sunnis, the differences mattered little in the ways Arab Muslims in France were represented. The nuances of Islam and the complexities of Iran were lost on television viewers, for whom chanting men and women clad in black chadors came to embody a difference that was not only cultural and religious but political. Those on the left, who had cheered Third World revolutions, found little to hope for in this religiously driven uprising; those on the right, who feared such revolutions, were confirmed in their hostility. Both sides converged on images of veiled women as emblematic of the loss of rights the Iranian revolution represented. Reports from Teheran of demonstrations against the imposition of the veil reinforced its association with women's oppression. Iran became for French observers a foil for their own republicanism, even though Iranian women vote and run for office and continue to have access to education and professional training, as well as to birth control and sex education. The distorted images of Iran, however, heightened the sense of an impossible divide between France and its immigrants. The divide was repeatedly documented in television coverage which turned the pathologies of individual Muslims in France into representative instances of this same alien "culture." Cases of forced marriage, and of one girl who was murdered by her brothers for going out with French men, were sensationalized and often linked to events in Iran. The behavior of delinquent youth in the suburbs—crime, drugs—began to be attributed to "immigrants." Immigrants were equated with North Africans (especially Algerians), who were equated with Arabs, who were equated with Muslims, whatever the religious beliefs of particular individuals. And the old portrayals of oversexed Arab men, violent and out of control, returned. This time though, the representation of Arab women was less ambiguous than in the past. Whereas they were depicted during the colonial period as both temptresses and victims, in this postcolonial moment they were most often seen as victims of Muslim patriarchy in general and of predatory Muslim boys in particular. In this way, the picture of the Muslim community as a homogeneous entity, dictating the lives of its female members, was systematically developed; its counterpoint was the individualism and gender equality of republican France.

Attempts were made to distinguish "good" Muslims from "bad," but these distinctions tended to get lost in the image that was developed by the media. Domestically, the increasing visibility, from 1983 on, of the National Front party, led by Jean-Marie Le Pen, fueled racist depictions of "immigrants," who "breed like rabbits" and will upset the "biological equilibrium."[50] Metaphors of conquest proliferated despite the efforts of antiracist groups formed to counter Le Pen's message and the attacks on immigrants that it provoked. *Figaro Magazine* devoted a special issue in October 1985 to the question, "Will We Still Be French in Thirty Years?" with a picture of a veiled Marianne (the symbol of the republic) on the cover. Gone was the mysterious sexuality that had so entranced colonial imaginations. Now the veil connoted envelopment or incorporation in a double sense: women were said to be coerced into wearing it by domineering men, and it was an ominous sign of a threatened takeover of France by Islamists.

The influence of external events on the perception of domestic immigrants was exacerbated by the Salman Rushdie affair in 1989 (when the Ayatollah Khomeini issued a fatwa against the author of *The Satanic Verses*) and then by the Gulf War in 1990–91. Despite major differences between Iran and Iraq, all were depicted as Arab Muslims, bloodthirsty fanatics with no respect for the laws of the West. The bicentennial of the French Revolution in 1989 then became the occasion for comparisons between republicanism and theocracy; Iran was portrayed as the inevitable embodiment of "Islam," and then "Islam" (with no qualifiers) was equated with Nazism and Communism. But it was the outbreak of civil war in Algeria that brought things to a head. An Islamist party won municipal elections in June 1990 and then the first round of legislative elections the following January. In response, the military government, fearing another Iran, canceled the elections with the support of France, and a brutal civil war ensued. From 1992 to 1995, Islamists not only attacked secular Algerians and French citizens in Algeria but also bombed buildings and railway stations within France. At the same time, and for reasons having to do with poverty and unemployment, riots spread through the impoverished North African suburbs outside of Paris and other cities. Although there was little evidence to connect them to Islamists either in Algeria or France, journalists nonetheless made these connections. Some even began to worry about a second Algerian War, which this time would be a war of conquest in a double sense: the conquest, not only of North African immigrants, but of France as a whole, by radical Islamists. In an odd way, the former status of Algeria—within France administratively, outside it geographically—was recalled in these images of an enemy state now within the metropole. In this context, it was no accident that De Gaulle's comment of

1959 (see pp. 61–62 above) was republished in the magazine
Le Point in 1994.

The imagined war pitted "the Muslim community" against
"France," as if each were a unified whole. France was treated as a
republic embodying universal values; the nation had no factions
or fissures. Muslims were likewise identified as a single community, a "culture" fixed in its practices, outside history. That there
were secular North Africans, that many who were called "immigrants" were in fact French citizens, that North African men
and women often took French spouses, that there were varieties
of religious practice and political affiliation among French
Muslims all seemed beside the point. Deltombe suggests there
would be outrage on the part of Catholics if the actions of the
Irish Republican Army, or for that matter of French fundamentalist Catholics, were attributed to a homogeneous "Catholic
community," but journalists and politicians had no hesitation
about treating Islam in this way.[51] Especially after attacks in
Paris by Islamists in 1995, the building of mosques was opposed by some local citizen groups, who defined these houses of
religion as enemy encampments. Instances of domestic violence
among Arabs became proof of the entire community's—the
culture's—dysfunction (while similar actions committed in
"French" households were treated as individual pathologies).
Disruptions in schools were deemed acts of provocation, and
difficult schools in immigrant neighborhoods were referred to
by some teachers as "lost territories" which must be retaken. A
new realism was called for in the face of the "communalist"
threat; those who refrained from criticism because of a misplaced leftism or a "bad conscience about colonialism" were
urged to "face the truth" about Muslims.[52]

The attacks on the World Trade Center in New York on September 11, 2001, exacerbated this Manichean view and introduced talk of a "clash of civilizations" into French political discourse. "It's Islam that has undertaken a crusade against the West, not the reverse," wrote one commentator.[53] The impossibility of integrating Muslims into French society became a kind of truism and the persistence of references to them as "newly arrived" or "immigrants" underscored their status as "foreigners," no matter how long they had lived in France. It was their liminality, in Bourdieu's sense, that was being confirmed. There were two immutable entities: Muslim "immigrants" and France. History and the changes associated with it were beside the point. "We live in a secular republic, where immigrants have freely chosen to settle," opined a writer in the newspaper *France Soir* in 2003. "They must adjust to our way of life, or they can go. Either one loves France or leaves it."[54] "What is shocking, irritating, and disconcerting," wrote two editors in *Le Nouvel Observateur*, "is that these guests of the state aren't polite enough to respect the laws of their hosts."[55] A French woman responding to a questionnaire in *Le Figaro* said, "It's necessary to subject yourself to the laws of the nation that welcomes you."[56] The language of "guest" and "host" obliterates entirely the structures of inequality on which the relationship rests. It assumes that free choice, not economic pressure, motivates these immigrants and it establishes a relationship of "us" and "them" that makes foreigners of Muslims, many of whom are already French citizens.

A friend told me of a conversation between two politicians during the debates about the passage of the headscarf law. "Frankly," said one—an eminent Jewish political figure—"these people can never be assimilated." Replied her colleague, "That's what used to be said about the Jews." The Jewish politician was terribly offended and adamantly refused the notion that racism might underlie her "realist" remark.

Jews in France

I want to pause for a moment to look at the history of Jews in France. Their situation has been different, of course, from that of Muslims, at least in part because Jews were not conquered colonial (and then postcolonial) subjects. Still, the history of French Jewry, from emancipation at the time of the French Revolution to the anti-Semitic laws of the Vichy regime, shows something of the way in which religion and race get intertwined, casting shadows on the universalist promise of assimilation as a way to Frenchness. Until after World War II, racial stigma attached to Jews no matter how secular and culturally French they became; as hard as they tried to assimilate, as successful as many were in commerce and the professions, they were rarely considered fully French.

The objection to enfranchising Jews in 1789 was that they constituted a community apart, a nation within a nation, because of their religious practices. "Everything must be refused to the Jews as a nation in the sense of a corporate body," declared Count Stanislas Clermont-Tonnerre, "and everything granted to the Jews as individuals. . . . They must make up neither a political body nor an order within the State; they must individually be citizens."[57] Most French Jews accepted this requirement of privatizing their religion even though seculariza-

tion did not proceed as rigidly as Clermont-Tonnerre suggested it should. (I will go into this in more detail in chapter
3.) As part of an attempt to subsume religion to state control,
Jewish religious institutions, like their Catholic and Protestant
counterparts, gained official recognition, and even state finan-
cial support during the nineteenth century.

For many French Jews assimilation was the route taken.
Some leaders urged more accommodation to French ways than
others, a few even proposing that the sabbath be moved to
Sunday; others abandoned religion entirely, embracing secularism and science in its place. Those who pushed for a synthesis
of progressive Jewish and French values asked to be designated
not French Jews—members of a separate collective culture
who were French by dint of geography—but Jews of France
(*français israélites*), individual French of Jewish ancestry who
were nonetheless full members of the national culture. Still,
historian Esther Benbassa tells us, those who carved out successful careers in politics and government met with discriminatory treatment; the state "considered them as members of a
close-knit group and not as full-fledged citizens."[58] Their Jew-
ishness—as much a racial as a religious trait—disqualified
them for the kind of equality espoused by republicans.

Currents of anti-Semitism ran deep in France, but they took
new form from the 1880s on as immigration accelerated from
Eastern Europe, bringing poorer Jews with different cultural
and religious practices into France. Despite the efforts of
French Jews to distinguish themselves from these Yiddish-
speaking, apparently clannish, and more religiously observant
newcomers, anti-Semites tarred them all with the same brush.
The Dreyfus Affair (1894–1906), in which a high level official

(in this case an army captain) was accused of treasonable actions, is the most famous of the incidents, but not the only one. The notion of an enemy within, the Jew as a representative of a foreign nation, was never far off. The prime minister of the Popular Front government (1936), Léon Blum, was variously depicted by right-wing nationalists as a Bolshevik agent, an enemy invader, or a cancer that must be expunged from the body of the nation. During the Vichy Regime (1940–44), as the French leadership fell in step with the German occupiers, laws restricting the movements and activities of Jews applied to "anyone who belongs to the Jewish religion or who belonged to it on 25 June 1940 and who is descended from two grandparents of the Jewish race."[59] Here race and religion were revealed as inseparable categories; the one implied the other.

In the aftermath of the Holocaust, many more French Jews embraced an identity they or their grandparents had shunned. Benbassa says the tendency was to think of oneself less as a Jewish French man, or woman (*français israélite*), than as a French Jew (*juif français*), with an emphasis now on a plural identity, one that in the United States we think of as a hyphenated identity. At the same time, successive governments were careful not to act in ways that might be considered anti-Semitic—the legacy of the Holocaust, when the French part in it was finally acknowledged, weighed, and still weighs, heavily. One can see it in antidiscrimination law, in laws that make it a crime to deny the Holocaust, and in the care which even nationalists like Le Pen take to avoid attacks on Jews.

The arrival of Jews from North Africa in the 1950s and 60s significantly changed the profile of French Jews. Like the Eastern Europeans before them, they are more visibly different,

more religious, less assimilated than their native French counterparts, though they speak French, coming as they do from
former colonies. They are more clearly members of a distinct
community that, like the Muslims', is bound by a religiosity
that impinges on all aspects of life. Women in these communities are required to dress in prescribed ways, to cover their
bodies and their hair; they pray separately from men and are
not considered men's equals. Until the headscarf law, Jewish
boys were allowed to wear skullcaps in public schools, although many (girls as well as boys) attend religious schools,
preferring a Jewish to a secular education. The Jews from the
Maghreb pose many of the same challenges to French universalism that Arabs/Muslims do, and yet the animus of those
who worry about the fracturing of the nation is directed at
Muslims, not at Jews. I'm not arguing that Jews should be tar-
geted; not at all. I do want to point out that one positive
legacy of France's history during the Second World War is a
decline in anti-Semitism, an admission of the wrongs committed because of that racism, and the acknowledgment that
the full integration of Jews is possible, even as some forms of
their identification newly stress a collective identity. Benbassa
puts it this way:

> various ways of being Jewish have emerged that testify to
> the pluralism and plurality of a group in the process of
> transforming itself [identifying as French Jews whatever
> their religious activity]. Moreover, open hostility toward
> Jews, the perception that they are different from others,
> and even reservations about the possibility that one day
> they might occupy the highest office in the land have vir-

tually disappeared since the liberation. Neither the tendency of government authorities to revert to a communitarian view of the Jewish collectivity nor the strengthening of collective identity and the willingness of certain Jewish leaders to move in the same direction is likely to call into question an established and solid integration.[60]

Although the conflicts in the Middle East, particularly Israel's treatment of Palestinians, has occasioned some attacks on Jews in recent years, this is hardly evidence of a resurgence of anti-Semitism. Instead, it is a misplaced attempt, usually by Palestinian sympathizers, to express opposition to Israel's policy of occupation. (It may also be a consequence of the insistence by defenders of Israeli policy that any criticism of Israel is anti-Semitic.) Despite these incidents, the social integration that Benbassa describes persists.

This was an integration that was not deemed possible in the years before and during World War II. It is an integration that many cannot foresee for Muslims, as the comment of the Jewish politician I cited demonstrates. Muslims are the primary target today for French racism. The terrible irony is that some Jews don't see the parallels to their own story.

Integration

The idea of a "clash of civilizations" played right into several decades of government policy that, while seeming to wrestle with the various ways to integrate North Africans into French society, actually entertained only one idea. The standard for becoming French remained what it had long been: assimilation.

And the characterization of Muslims as unassimilable persisted alongside it.

Throughout the nineteenth and most of the twentieth century, France was a society of immigrants; it received more foreign-born people than any other Western country, including
the United States. Unlike the United States, however, which,
under the sign of what came to be called multiculturalism, professed accommodation of the ethnic and religious diversity of
newcomers, France required its immigrants to conform to existing cultural norms. There is no less discrimination and conflict in the United States than in France, perhaps even more
hypocrisy here, but the legal and philosophical differences do
seem to matter for the ways discrimination can be challenged.
If the motto of the United States is *e pluribus unum*, in France
it is "the nation, one and indivisible." "One and indivisible"
means, quite literally, that differences cannot be formally recognized; no official statistics are kept on the ethnicities or religions of the population. If differences are not documented,
they do not exist from a legal point of view, and so they do not
have to be tolerated, let alone celebrated.

This does not mean that policymakers were unaware of the
growing problems of poverty and social dislocation among
North African populations; they were, of course. These immigrants, who make up about 8 percent of the population, account for about a third of all unemployed. They are last hired
and first fired; the rates of unemployment of fifteen- to
twenty-four-year-olds of Algerian origin, even those with
school diplomas, are more than double those of "native"
French with the same credentials. As in the 1920s and 30s, the
problems are framed in terms of intractable cultural differences

rather than socioeconomic conditions. Here the paradox of the old civilizing mission reappears: it is most often the "culture" of North Africans that is blamed for their social marginalization, a "culture" that precludes their integration into French society. Deltombe offers examples of television commentators who remarked on the strangeness of these foreigners and the way their behavior strained "thresholds of tolerance" among the French; the implication was that North Africans caused the racism they so resented. The conclusion, repeatedly, was that unless North Africans gave up Islam they could not become French. "France is the site of an exciting venture," commented Jean Daniel, the founding editor of *Le Nouvel Observateur,* "that of transforming Islam through its contact with French civilization."[61]

The civilizing process, once the justification for colonialism, was now to be applied to immigrants; former colonial subjects were to be integrated as French nationals. According to a theory of integration, articulated by policymakers in the 1980s and early 1990s, cultural differences were private (and secondary) commitments that must have nothing to do with an individual's primary identification as a member of the French nation. Following recommendations from an advisory body formed to address "integration," and in the context of a series of laws passed to tighten controls over "foreigners" living in France, the government revised the code of nationality in 1993 and stipulated that citizenship would no longer be extended as a matter of course to children born in France of foreign-born parents. These second-generation residents now had to ask to become citizens, indicating their desire as individuals to enter the social contract and their willingness to put communal loy-

alties aside. Further, children of Algerians who were born before independence (when Algeria was still French), needed to
supply proof of "enracinement" (rootedness, which also had
overtones of assimilatedness) in order to qualify for a citizenship that had once been a matter of course. To become a citizen, a report in 1993 stated, meant enjoying full freedom of
private communal association and explicitly rejecting "the logic
of there being distinct ethnic or cultural minorities, and instead looking for a logic based on the equality of individual
persons."[62] It was only as individuals, then, that Arabs could
become fully French. (The emphasis on individuals, a key to
republican ideology, continued after the Socialists returned to
power in 1997 even when they dropped the required proof of
"enracinement.")

   The problem with this policy was that North Africans were
already defined as members of communities and discriminated
against in those terms. They lived in separate enclaves on the
edges of cities, at once invisible and visibly distinct from residents of city centers. Geographic segregation gave literal
boundaries to these "communities," but they also hid the many
differences among the Arabs and Muslims who lived in them.
How could individuals shed communal characteristics that
were *attributed to them* because of their country of origin, or
their parents' country of origin, or the place they now lived, or
the names that marked them? How could individuals privately
embrace Islam as a religion without raising the suspicion that
"communal identities" defined their entire lives? Which practices were expressions of private commitment? Weren't there
still cultural norms setting the terms of who counted as an individual? A girl in a headscarf was a member of a "community,"

but a girl in a miniskirt was expressing her individuality—was this an objective distinction, or one which rested on normative standards in the guise of neutrality? "Integration" did not address these thorny dilemmas; instead it reproduced the opposition between communal Muslims and individualist French and the racist logic upon which that opposition rested. "These young North Africans, sons of immigrants . . . today feel more French than Muslim," commented one hopeful journalist.[63] The choice was clear: only by giving up all signs of belonging to the Islamic faith could these people become "fully French," and even then all sorts of differences (propensities to crime and sexual excess, religious zealotry and laziness, "traditional" customs and beliefs) might keep them on the margins of the society of which they were already a part. Although a minority among French intellectuals had offered a plan for integration that called for a recognition of the reality of differences in the population, defining them as components of a mosaic nation, their plan was rejected by the majority as being too close to American multiculturalism. American multiculturalism was chaotic and divisive; it was antithetical to French universalism, which created a nation whose unity rested on seeing each person only as an individual.

There were, to be sure, representatives of "moderate" Islam whose opinions gained a hearing; the head of the Paris mosque, for example, repeatedly made it clear that terrorism was not endorsed by most of his followers. None of this was enough to achieve full acceptance for Muslims; even moderate Islam seemed to carry the taint of extremism. The controversial Swiss scholar Tariq Ramadan suggested not only that Islam could coexist with a secular state but also that there might

be such a thing as Islamic feminism. He was attacked as disin-
genuous by some French feminists, who claimed that he said
one thing to French audiences in French, quite another when
he spoke to Muslims in Arabic. Even if this charge is true (and
I have no evidence either way), the point I want to make is
that these feminists take Islam to be necessarily antithetical to
feminism.

Nowhere was the refusal to grant credibility to any form of
Islam more evident than in the headscarf controversies which
erupted in 1989, 1994, and 2003 (and which I detailed in the
last chapter). There could be no such thing, in the eyes of the
vast majority of French, as a moderate Muslim wearing a veil.
"The veil is a terrorist operation," commented philosopher André Glucksmann in the pages of *L'Express* in 1994.[64] In his eyes
it was a sign not of personal religious commitment (as a yarmulke might be for a Jewish boy) but of defiance—a deliberate
refusal of integration, an unwillingness to become French.
"Like it or not," President Jacques Chirac stated in 2003,
"wearing a veil is a kind of aggression."[65] Here we find an echo
of General Bugeaud's comment as he led the conquest of Algeria in the 1840s ("the Arabs elude us because they conceal their
women from our gaze"). Jean Daniel, whose politics are to the
left of Chirac's, nevertheless condemned those who would permit the veil: "Anticolonialism," he wrote, "led us to tolerate differences. Republican patriotism ought to demand a search for
sameness."[66] In other words, unless "they" become exactly like
"us," integration is not possible and, by definition, "they" are
not "us" and can never become "us."

Perhaps the most dramatic example of the persistence of
the old colonial "civilizing mission" came during a television
debate in January 2004, which featured Saïda Kada, founder of

Femmes françaises et musulmanes engagées (French Muslim Women in Action), who herself wears a headscarf and defends it as a form of religious, not political, expression, and Elisabeth Badinter, a staunch advocate of "the values of the Republic." Insisting that the headscarf was not antithetical to women's freedom but in fact represented an individual choice, Kada urged greater understanding of Islam: "I think today two things are mixed up together [that ought to be separated]: emancipation and Westernization." An agitated Badinter broke in: "Rightly so; they are rightly connected to one another."[67] In her comment there is a fascinating slippage from "Westernization" to the emancipatory values of republican France and from there, tacitly, to modernity. For Badinter, "France" is the highest embodiment of the Western and the modern.

The Law of February 23, 2005

As if to deny the argument put forth by critics of the government policy of integration, that a new "respectable racism" characterized the treatment of immigrants, a law was passed, quietly and without much fanfare, early in 2005. Its aim was to attract pied noir voters by expressing the gratitude of the nation "to the women and men who participated in the work accomplished by France" in the former territories of Algeria, Morocco, Tunisia, and Indochina, to "recognize their suffering and their sacrifices" as administrators and soldiers in the colonies and after repatriation, and to provide remuneration to their descendants. There would be a memorial established to those who died fighting for France in the colonial wars in North Africa. Singled out for special recognition and for protection against "insults and defamation" were the *harkis*, a minority of Algerians who had fought on the side of the French.[68] Here were "Arabs" or "Muslims" whose political allegiance would finally be recognized. (The law did not manage to overcome local hostilities: in 2005 the mayor of the city of Montpellier, referred to the harkis as "sous hommes" [subhumans].)

The most surprising part of the law, and one that drew a petition of protest from a number of established historians, was article 4, which addressed scholarly research and university teaching on the subject of colonialism. "Programs of university research will accord to the history of the French overseas presence, notably in North Africa, the attention it merits. Scholarly programs will particularly recognize the positive role played by the French presence overseas, notably in North Africa, and grant to this history and to the sacrifices of the combatants in the French army who came from these territories the place of preeminence to which they have a right."[69]

The protesting historians rejected this kind of "official history" because it was "contrary to scholarly neutrality and to liberty of thought." They argued, too, that by insisting only on a "positive role" for colonialization, the law gave "official lie" to the "crimes, massacres that often amounted to genocide, slavery, and racism" that were the legacy of this past. Although some journalists suspected that the passage of the law was the work of a pied noir lobby that had taken advantage of a lull in legislative activity to put forward a bill that they knew the conservative government would endorse, the comment of the historians seems more to the point. The law, they said, "legalizes a nationalist communalism that will elicit in response a communalism from groups whose past history will have been denied." Put in other terms, the historians feared that the law would only antagonize further the North Africans who were the object of discrimination—a discrimination linked to their status as former colonial subjects. It would pit France against its "immigrants," intensifying resentments and estrangements on both sides, not only because the North Africans would be denied the validity of their historical experience, but also because there would be no way to convince "France" of the need to come to terms with it.[70]

The law of February 23, 2005, was one of those amazing moments in which an official action designed to conceal something actually reveals what it most wants to hide: in this case the fact that the colonial past, with its legacy of discrimination against, and denigration of, North Africans, continued to trouble the nation in ways that seemed endless and insoluble. It was as if in the absence of a real solution, there was nothing left to do but repress the problem. The difficulty, of course, is not only that the repressed invariably returns but that it does so through symptoms that then create their own disturbances. Rather than do away with the controversy created by the headscarf ban in 2004, the law of February 23, 2005, exposed the ban's underlying motives: the desire to eliminate rather than address the growing challenge to French republicanism posed by the aftermath of its colonial history. It could be argued that the riots by disaffected suburban youth in the fall of 2005 proved that denying the challenge did not make it go away.

Conclusion

Despite recent attempts to efface it, the legacy of colonialism persists. It extended well beyond the end of the French empire; its traces are visible today in debates about the status of "immigrant" Arab/Muslim populations. Even the term "immigrant," used to refer to North Africans (and sometimes, too, to West Africans from former French colonies, but never to those who have "European" origins), no matter how long ago they arrived in France, signals not only their current lack of integration but the impossibility of its ever happening. The paradox of a civilizing mission aimed at the uncivilizable continues. Even if the characteristics attributed to French North Africans have changed over the years, the stigma of their origin still attaches to them. Although many are legally citizens, few have made it into the upper echelons particularly of politics and the professions. One recent and highly publicized case involved protests (including death threats) against the appointment of a Muslim as a prefect (roughly equivalent to a governor)—the first of his kind to be selected for such a post. Discrimination is a big problem. During the 2005 riots, it was pointed out that few Arabs had ever been hired as police, though such a presence might have diminished the sense of embattlement in ghetto neighborhoods. Also during those riots, some commentators initially offered "Islam" as an explanation for an uprising of displaced, impoverished youth who expressed little or no religious motivation for their actions. In a kind of perverse logic and despite evidence to the contrary, this urban unrest (and so the failure of these "immigrant" youth to integrate) was at first attributed to Islam (by definition, not susceptible to integration). The ethnic/religious identification, the thing that makes these "Muslims" from North Africa eternally inferior, is their presumed religion; when they actually do embrace Islam, it becomes further proof that, whatever the technicalities of their formal citizenship, they can never be fully French. Here in new form is the ongoing tension that marked the "civilizing mission" from the outset. On the one hand, the promise of inclusion is held out to those who choose to become French; on the other hand, the very characteristics that mark these people as in need of "civilizing" prevent their ever realizing the promise. For what sustains the superiority of the French, what makes them civilizers (instead of oppressors) is the inferiority of those they seek to uplift.

I have argued in this chapter that the veil in French republican discourse is understood in racist terms, whether it connotes excessive sexuality or a denial of sexuality, whether it is worn as an expression of personal religious commitment or as a sign of political opposition. From the earliest days of conquest through decolonization and its aftermath, the veil has figured as a potent political emblem. It has conjured up fantasies of domination and submission as well as of seduction and terror; for some it is an expression of agency, for others a sign of victimization, and for many a practical instrument of warfare. That the veil continues to be at issue in France's struggle to come to terms with its colonial past and its ethnically mixed population in the present ought not to be surprising. Drawing the line at the wearing of the veil is a way of drawing the line not only at Islam but at the differences Arab and Muslim populations represent, a way of insisting on the timeless superiority of French "civilization" in the face of a changing world.

3

SECULARISM

Racism was the subtext of the headscarf controversy, but secularism was its explicit justification. The law prohibiting "conspicuous" signs of religious affiliation in public schools was defined above all as a defense of "laïcité," "the cornerstone" of French republicanism, the principle that clearly separated church from state. Headscarves were deemed an intrusion of religion into the sacred secular space of the schoolroom, the crucible in which French citizens are formed. What was at stake, supporters of the ban argued, was nothing less than the future of the nation, the unity of the social body. "Etymologically," began the National Assembly report (*Secularism and Schools*), "laïcité designates the *laos*, the people considered as an indivisible whole."[1] Although the report conceded that the private rights of individual conscience must be respected and that the neutrality of the state must be maintained in relation to the diversity of religious beliefs among its population, these could not outweigh considerations of national unity. In any contest between individual rights and state sovereignty, the interests of the state must prevail.

Despite firm assertions of this kind, however, the headscarf controversy opened a searing debate about the meanings of French secularism, the limits of religious toleration, and the founding principles of the republic. Proponents of a law to ban headscarves insisted that it would only enforce long-established boundaries between the public and the private, the political and the religious. In fact, the debates showed these boundaries to be anything but clear. It was the lack of clarity—and a sense of desperate need for it—that defined the situation as a crisis.

Although the French case must be understood in terms of its specific history, the issues at stake have larger significance. These days many of us find ourselves confronted with challenges to what we have taken to be long-established principles of social and political organization. Secularism is one of those principles. Roughly speaking, the word denotes the separation of church and state, but beyond that there are historical differences in its meaning and implementation. In America, home to religious minorities who fled persecution at the hands of European rulers, the separation between church and state was meant to protect religions from unwarranted government intervention; the First Amendment to the Constitution begins "Congress shall make no law respecting an establishment of religion, or prohibiting the free exercise thereof." This was designed to prevent any single religion from dominating the affairs of state, and it was soon extended to keep religiosity as such out of government. In France, separation was intended to secure the allegiance of individuals to the republic and so break the political power of the Catholic church. There the state claimed the undivided loyalty of citizens to the nation, and that meant relegating to a private sphere the claims of religious communities. This was expressed as state protection of individuals from the claims of religion. In France, the state protects individuals from religion; in America, religions are protected from the state and the state from religion. But in both cases, the terrain of politics is meant to be free of religious influence; it is considered essential to republican democracy that religion is a private affair. The distinction between private and public (religious belief and one's obligations to the state) is based in traditions historically associated with Christianity.

Now, often in the name of democracy, members of religious groups have begun to demand recognition of their particular beliefs and interests and have defined secularism as an obstacle to the full enjoyment of their rights as citizens. Moreover, some of them—Christian fundamentalists in the United States, for example—go further, seeking to deny the secular basis of the state altogether and insisting upon a "return" to the "original" religious beliefs of the founding fathers. To this end, they have produced a stream of revisionist scholarship designed to prove that the American constitution is rooted not in Enlightenment universalism but in Christian revelation.

Even as secularism has been assaulted from the right, it has also been criticized from the left by those who see it both as a way in which states have created acceptable forms of religion (in this sense it is a "regulatory practice") and as a mask for the political domination of "others," a form of ethnocentrism or crypto-Christianity, the particular product of the history of the European nation-state. Its claim to universalism (a false universalism in the eyes of its critics) has justified the exclusion or marginalization of those from non-European cultures (often immigrants from former colonies) whose systems of belief do not separate public and private in the same way, do not, in other words, conform to those of the dominant group. Writes the political theorist William Connolly in a book provocatively titled *Why I Am Not a Secularist*, "Democratic governance readily degenerates into the organization of unity through the demoralization of otherness."[2] And this (as we shall see in this chapter) certainly captures something of what was going on in the headscarf controversy. The law insisted on the unacceptable difference (the "otherness") of those whose personal/religious identity was achieved by wearing the hijab, even though these girls did not seek to impose their beliefs on their schoolmates but simply insisted that they themselves could not dress in any other way without a loss of their sense of identity.

From my American perspective, the French case is an argument against secularism, proof of Connolly's point that its effect can be intolerance and discrimination. From the French side, however, the growing political strength of evangelical Christians in the United States is proof of exactly the opposite: the urgent need for a strong secular state. If Christian moralism, presented as revealed truth, is allowed to dictate standards of behavior for everyone, if as a result the right-to-life trumps the right-to-choose, they say, then democracy as we have known it is lost. This is an argument I agree with. So it seems I am caught in an impossible dilemma: for or against secularism? Is the principle too easily corrupted, as the French case suggests? Or does it necessarily protect us from religious absolutism? Is it possible to separate an abstract ideal from its concrete history and from the political uses to which it is put? Are these questions themselves an indication of what one anthropologist has called an "impasse of liberalism," the exhaustion of Enlightenment beliefs in the context of a new global world? Or do they walk into what the philosopher Slavoj Žižek warns is a trap that forecloses politics by thinking of abstract universal principles only in concrete terms?[3]

Part of my difficulty in sorting this out comes from the fact that secularism is *both* the product of the particular histories of Christian Western European nation-states and a principle claimed to be universal. The invocation of the principle always does specific historical work, so it's hard to endorse it abstractly. Yet it is precisely the abstraction that provides the grounds for arguing specific cases: keeping creationism out of the public school curriculum in the United States or banning Islamic headscarves in French public schools. In order to distinguish between these two instances, we have to look at concrete outcomes: in the first case, it's what all children are taught that's at issue; in the second, it's the right of a small group of children to be taught what everyone else is learning despite the personal religious identification their clothing proclaims. Of course, secularism figures in both cases: in the first, it rules out claims of religious truth in the public school curriculum; in the second, it requires that there be no sign of student religious affiliation in a public school. But there's something about the democratic result of the process that's important too: in the first case, a minority is prevented from dictating its religious belief to a majority; in the second, a minority is denied access, on the grounds of its religious belief, to what the majority enjoys. Perhaps it's the democratic outcomes I'm interested in more than the principle of secularism itself.

But even if that is the case, secularism—as it is now often invoked in Western European countries confronting Muslim populations in their midst—carries connotations that must be addressed because they structure the way we think about how to deal with religion in general and Islam in particular. Typically, secularism is equated with modernity and religion with tradition. Both as history and principle, secularism is taken to be a sign of modernity, the opening to democracy, the triumph of reason and science over superstition, sentiment, and unquestioned belief. The state becomes modern, in this view, by suppressing or privatizing religion because it is taken to represent the irrationality of tradition, an obstacle to open debate and discussion. Religion is associated with the past; the secular state with the present and future. So in some areas outside of the West, religion has been forcibly privatized (if not outlawed altogether) and secularism embraced as a national route to modernity. This was the case in Turkey in 1923, in Iran in 1936 under the rule of the shah, and in India at the moment of its independence in 1947. For the Soviet Union and its satellite states, secularism was officially mandated, associated, like socialism, with the progress of history.

Yet if we take a comparative international perspective, we find there are modern states that are not secular and religions that are not traditional. There are secular states that are not democratic—that forbid any dissent—and religions whose law is the result of ongoing interpretative debate. Not only do religions have a rationality and a logic of their own that belies the "traditional" characterization of them, but they have evolved over time; their theologians and jurists have reinterpreted founding texts in relation to changing social, economic, and political conditions. In a like manner, many states have secularized by recognizing the religious beliefs of their citizens and finding ways to accommodate them, sometimes by declaring religious holidays as state holidays (the Sunday Sabbath in Christian countries is a prime example), sometimes by consulting religious leaders about the impact on their followers of proposed legislation, sometimes by including religious blocs in the allocation of seats in a parliament. This treatment of religion by secular states is the result not just of pragmatic adaptation aimed at regulation (though it surely is that) but also of the interpretation and reinterpretation of the principle of secularism in particular and changing contexts.

Instead of positing religion as the antithesis of secularism (particularly its democratic forms), it's useful to see that they also sometimes operate as parallel systems of interpretation. This can certainly be said of some Protestant denominations as well as of Judaism and Islam, where there is neither institutional centralization nor a singular head of the church. Both democratic states and these religions refer to founding texts (constitutions, divine revelation, bodies of law), both delegate to experts (lawyers, judges, theologians) authority to reconcile text and interpretation, but both also open to more general, lay discussion the meanings of the laws which set rules for behavior and the expression of belief. I don't want to push the analogy too far, just far enough to offer an alternative to the characterization of religion as an obstacle both to democracy and change. I don't deny that in secular states the relationship between the political and the religious is asymmetrical, that democratic states have coercive power that exceeds any influence religion may have, but the importance of interpretation is still worth noting. Thinking this way opens the relationship between the state and its religions to negotiation without either forcibly repressing religion or giving up on democracy—which remains a place where political resolution is never achieved on the ground of religious truth. And it more accurately reflects the historical processes by which the Christian nations of Western Europe modernized. In those nations, the principle of secularism might be described historically as one which protects the political sphere from the determining influence of a dominant religion while recognizing religion's public (social, cultural) importance—it is not only a private, individual matter.

According to this definition—which gives priority to history and yet recognizes the power of argument from principle—France's drawing the line at Islam in the name of secularism involved a distortion of that nation's own history. Or perhaps it is better to say that a particular idea of secularism—conceived in sharp oppositional terms as the expulsion of religion from the public sphere—became an ideological tool in an anti-Muslim campaign. It was another way of putting Muslim populations outside the bounds of "France" by deeming their religion and their culture not only unacceptably different but dangerous.

Laïcité

French supporters of the law banning headscarves defined themselves as apostles of secularism. This was not just any secularism but a special French version, at once more universal than any other *and* unique to French history and French national character ("une singularité française"). This secularism insisted on its truth (and on the danger that religion, a false truth, posed to it). As I mentioned at the outset of this chapter, laïcité refers not simply to separation of church and state but to the role of the state in protecting individuals from the claims of religion. It further rests on the notion that the secular and the sacred can be divided in the lives of individuals. Matters of individual conscience are private and should be free from public interference; the state's job is to protect that privacy. Unlike other secular democracies, wrote Bernard Stasi in the introduction to his commission's report, "France has raised laïcité to the level of a founding value."[4] The language of Stasi and his colleagues revealed the absolutist nature of their beliefs and their fervent nationalism. The school was a "sacred" space; secularism was "un méta-idéal humain";[5] the headscarf ban was necessary to prevent a takeover of the school by "the street." The battle was cast as a veritable "crisis," a war to the death between polar opposites: in abstract terms, between the republic and religion, modernity and tradition, reason and superstition; in concrete terms, between contemporary France and Islam. The image of a final conflict between truth and error deliberately invoked past efforts to wrest control of the hearts and minds of citizens from the spiritual and institutional power of the Catholic church, even though Muslims are a small minority with nothing comparable to the social power which organized Catholicism still wields. In fact, repeated references to the purely secular nature of the nation so misrepresented the history of its accommodations with the Catholic church that opponents of the ban charged supporters with hypocrisy. The issue, the critics maintained, was not religion in general but Islam, and not just Islam but "immigrants." In the end, they argued, the defense of secularism was but another mask for racism.

Historically, laïcité in schools dated to the Third Republic's

Ferry laws (1881–82, 1886), which made primary education compulsory for boys and girls and which effectively banished from the classroom religion as a subject and priests and nuns as teachers. It is important to note that the laws did not expel children who professed the Catholic faith, went to church on Sunday, or wore crosses and other religious medallions to class. "They had no obligation to conceal their religious affiliations."[6] The successful effort to wrest control from the Catholic church—which was considered an enemy of the republic, allied to monarchists who still nurtured dreams of another Bourbon Restoration—defined the school as the place where national unity would be forged, where the children of peasants (who spoke a variety of regional dialects and usually followed the instructions of a priest) would become patriots.[7] From the perspective of minister of education Jules Ferry, the school was to be the agent of assimilation; the goal of its pedagogy was to instill a common republican political identity in children from a diversity of backgrounds. The school was to effect a transition from private to public, from the world of the locality and the family to that of the nation. Teachers were the crucial element in this process—secular missionaries, charged with converting their pupils to the wonders of science and reason and the reasonableness of republican principles. A shared language, culture, and ideological formation—and so a nation one and indivisible—was to be the *outcome* of the educational process. Schools were the instruments for constructing the nation, not embodiments of the nation itself. And they had enormous authority, for they were the privileged site where differences were contained and transformed into Frenchness.

Militantly secular in theory, French schools were more flexible in practice, in part because of their belief in the power of reason to prevail in the educational process, in part because the state recognized the historic significance of Catholicism. The public schools accommodated the desire of parents (and the pressure of churches) for children to have religious education and treated it as a right. Even after the separation of church and state was mandated by law in 1905, students were not expected to attend classes on Sunday, and they were given another day off so they could receive religious instruction in their churches. In this way, the importance of religion in their formation was recognized, even as it was defined as an extracurricular activity, not part of the education they received at school. (The secular state also maintains religious buildings as a public responsibility; this is true not only of Christian churches, but of the Paris Mosque, built in 1926 to commemorate the deaths of Muslim soldiers in World War I.)

Although the constitutions of the Fourth and Fifth Republics (1946, 1958) define France as an "indivisible, secular, democratic, and social republic," this has not prevented state support of religious schools. Since 1958, the French government has contributed 10 percent of the budgets of private religious schools; more than 2 million children attend state-supported Catholic schools. (One Muslim school was recently established after eight years of difficult negotiation.) In 1984, when the government of President Mitterrand proposed integrating these schools into a unified, secular system, massive demonstrations were held in defense of "l'école libre," and the project was abandoned. The school calendar still observes only Catholic (Christmas, Easter, etc.) and state holidays; the proposal of the Stasi commission to add a Jewish and Muslim holiday was rejected by President Chirac. A former minister of education agreed with this decision on the grounds that the addition of Jewish and Muslim holidays would encourage religious "communalism" in otherwise secular schools. For him the Christian holidays don't violate the principle of secularism—proof to critics of "laïcité" that it is not universal at all but is, rather, intimately bound up with the dominant Catholic religious culture of the nation.

In some areas, historical circumstances have led to even more dramatic compromises with religion, compromises the Stasi commission was, in the name of "history," loath to touch in 2003. The three departments of Alsace-Moselle, lost at the conclusion of the Franco-Prussian War in 1871 and regained after World War I, have never been required to conform to the terms of the pact of 1905, nor were the colonies, where all sorts of bargains were struck with local religious authorities. In Alsace-Moselle religious instruction (for Catholics, Lutherans, Calvinists, and Jews) is still a mandatory part of the public school curriculum. With the permission of their parents, children who do not want to take these classes may substitute courses in morality. Rather than require the application of laïcité to schools in these departments (and so a genuinely universal policy), the Stasi commission recommended only that, in the name of fairness, religious instruction be added for Muslims.

Even as it acknowledged the inconsistencies of its recommendations (and justified them on the grounds of respect for the wishes of the local population in Alsace-Moselle, the preponderant influence of Christianity in French history, and the historical variability of the concept of laïcité itself), even as it insisted that secularism was in no way dogmatic, the Stasi commission presented laïcité as a principle that allowed for no negotiation with religion[8]—at least, no negotiation with "extremist groups," who are "testing the resistance of the Republic and pushing some young people to reject . . . its values."[9] Minimizing the long struggle with militant Catholics in earlier centuries and the tremendous controversies over the assimilability of Jews, the Stasi report deemed Islam a special case. It was not only historically outside the original "pacte laïque" of 1905 but also less willing to accommodate its dogmas to the requirements of a pluralist society. Granting that there were some more "rational" Muslims who understood the difference between political and spiritual power, the report nonetheless assumed that most followers of Islam would reject this distinction.[10] Thus "extremist groups" became typical of Islam as a whole and since their Islam, by definition, didn't recognize the values of liberty and laïcité, there was no need to tolerate Islam.[11] The fantasy of a crusading Islam wedded to an unalterable "truth" became the justification for—and the mirror of— an absolutist, intransigent secularism. The commission's report pitted France against its Muslims as homogeneous, warring categories, and ruled out the possibility that girls in headscarves might be rational agents who dressed according to deeply held personal religious beliefs.

The odd thing about the Stasi report—indeed about the argument of all those who favored the prohibition of headscarves in schools—was that it took integration to be a *prerequisite* for education, rather than its outcome. Proponents of the law insisted that students had to come to school as individuals; what communal identities they had must be left at home. In effect, Jules Ferry's vision of the school as the crucible of citizenship, the space of transition from private to public, from family and community to nation, was replaced; the school now became a miniature version of the nation, conceived as a collection of abstract individuals who were shorn of any identity other than their French citizenship. As in the representative bodies of the nation, so in the schools, universalism meant conformity to the same rules, and membership in only one "cult," the republic. Those who did not conform *in advance*, who were not already "French," fell outside the purview of the universal because, as in the body of the nation, commonality was a prerequisite for membership in the educational community. In the impeccable logic of former minister of education Bayrou: "The school is designed to integrate; therefore it must exclude."[12] This was another way of saying that Muslims could never be French.

Those who believed that Muslims should be considered members of the nation had a different notion of laïcité and its history. For them the school must necessarily reflect the actual diversity of society; its job was to negotiate differences and to create some commonality through the shared experience of education. It was the mythologized secularism of proponents of the law, they suggested, that created a crisis, not the fact that a few girls wore headscarves to school. These opponents of the ban insisted that integration was a gradual process with its own "temporal logic." "To ask young Muslim women to take off their veils before coming to class is a bit like asking them to pass final exams at the beginning of the course."[13] In an ideal classroom, there would be respect for diversity, achieved through a notion of neutrality, as well as the possibility for children to become autonomous subjects. If autonomy meant rejecting the pressures of religion and family, so much the better, but it might also just mean simply understanding the choices others have urged you to make.

Underlying many of the statements opposing the law were the same commitments that seemed to drive the law's proponents: to education as a modernizing process and to secularism as a way of containing the power of religious truth claims. There were, though, important differences. For one, critics of the law argued that assimilation was the wrong model for national unity; there could be toleration and coexistence of differences without homogenization. Indeed, if secularism were understood as a platform for the negotiation of difference instead of as its erasure, national unity based on shared values might still be the result. The question was how to have a "dynamic process of integration" that was not "a policy of pure and simple assimilation."[14] What better place than a public school to stage the "encounter of cultures and values" that might produce a new universalism?[15] In this vision, the school was the training ground for secularism, a preparation for participation in adult politics, a place in which the merits of ideas would be weighed without regard for their provenance. In addition, although there was no question that the state would continue to set limits and standards for religious expression (as it did for education), Christianity would not be the sole model for determining the acceptability of other religions. According to this form of secularism, children who refused to take history courses which contradicted their religious views would be ruled out of order, while those wearing headscarves (or other indicators of religious commitment) would not. The critical point was that the privatization of belief was not required as proof of eligibility for school attendance, or, for that matter, of eligibility for membership in the national community.

The debate about the meaning of secularism between supporters and opponents of the headscarf ban was uneven, to put it mildly. Although the outpouring of opposition to the law consumed many pages of newspapers, journals and books, its public impact was muted by the stridency of the law's supporters, who represented a considerable majority and who argued in stark either/or terms. There was little room for the kind of nuance—philosophical or historical—offered by opponents of the law. As debate escalated and the foulard became synonymous with the voile, you were either pro- or anti-veil. Those who insisted that Muslim girls should continue to be admitted to public school were quickly labeled "pro-veil" (and in some instances, dangerous Islamists), even when they took pains to insist on their commitment to laïcité and to distance themselves from religious apologists. So, for example, an appeal by a group of intellectuals and activists originally entitled "Yes to Laïcité, No to Laws of Exclusion" appeared in the newspaper *Libération* on May 20, 2003, with a new title not approved by the authors: "Yes to the Headscarf in Secular Schools."[16] (The change reflected the pro-exclusion stance taken by the editors of this left-leaning newspaper.) Many of these same intellectuals chose to resign from the board of the feminist journal *Pro-Choix* when they were denounced by its editors as supporters of "fundamentalism." They were also depicted as "partisans of the veil."[17] The Stasi commission report, like the one produced by the National Assembly study group, was largely devoted to the testimony of experts about the meaning of the veil and about

the ways in which Islam and radical Islamists were responsible
for all sorts of disruptions in the schools. Despite many nuanced testimonies—about the multiple meanings of the headscarf, about social and economic discrimination against North
Africans, and about the crises of finance and authority in the
schools themselves—the conclusion of these official bodies was
that banning the veil was the only way to contain the crisis that
Islam had unleashed and the best way to enforce the secular
aims of the republic. The falsehoods of Islam must not be allowed to dilute the hard truth of French laïcité. In this way, one
absolutism was offered to counter another, and the door was
shut to the kind of political conversation that was needed if the
urgent social problems of the Arab/Muslim "immigrant" population were to be addressed. Indeed, I would argue that in this
case, the dominant conception of laïcité was as unbending as
the Islam it purported to combat.

The School

The law forbidding headscarves in primary and secondary
public schools was a symbolic gesture in the war of the republic
against its enemy. It was not as if all headscarves were banned
from all public places. Private schools, which receive subven-
tions from the state, were not governed by the ban. Women in
the street were allowed to dress as they chose, as were university students, who were considered free agents. And, as many
critics pointed out, women with headscarves were allowed to
go on cleaning schools and government offices without being
considered a danger to the foundations of the secular state. Although the law was worded so as to have universal application

(it banned all conspicuous religious signs), nobody until now had worried about Jewish boys wearing skullcaps or Sikhs wearing turbans. The law was applied to them as a kind of afterthought and without provoking any debate. Why was school attire so important? And why direct a law primarily at underage Muslim girls?

The answer to these questions, as I have already indicated, is that since the Third Republic, schools have been considered the key to disseminating and stabilizing republicanism, to creating France as a nation one and indivisible. Under the Ferry laws, children were the target population for cultivating and reproducing republican values, and girls were particularly important to reach if the power of priests over women (a power thought to be so strong that it justified denying women the vote until 1945) was to be broken. The old concern about women and religion (and the state's particular responsibility for the weaker sex) was transposed in 2003 onto Islam but with a twist: Muslim girls stood in for all vulnerable children, and the supposed pressure from their fathers, brothers, and imams to wear headscarves recalled the once formidable power of Catholic priests. At the same time, girls in headscarves embodied the very peril from which vulnerable children needed to be protected: they carried the virus, as it were, of religion into the school. To further complicate things, they were perceived as making a statement about sexuality that was also considered out of place (see chapter 5).

The Stasi commission took its recommendations to be an affirmation of the Ferry laws, but it did not acknowledge the vast changes that had taken place in schools since the golden age of the Third and Fourth Republics. Schools no longer enjoyed the same prestige or performed the same functions. Moreover, society had changed as well; there was a deeper racial divide than ever before, exacerbated by the seeming unwillingness of political leaders to do anything about it. Schools were the microcosm of a society under siege, not because of a challenge to secularism by religious students and their parents, but because of many economic and social factors, including what the sociologist of education François Dubet calls a process of "massification."[18] This involved the entry, from the 1970s on, of vast numbers of lower-class students into secondary schools (the four year *collèges* and then the *lycées*, equivalent to our middle and high schools), accompanied by changes in the schools' mission, the role of teachers, and the relation between schools and society. In his account—which I will rely on in what follows—it is class (compounded in some instances by race) and not religion, that is the heart of the matter. The headscarf law was, from this perspective, a displacement of concern, a way to avoid facing the social and economic dilemmas that roiled French schools.

Although the Ferry laws of the 1880s made primary education secular and compulsory, in fact just a small portion of the population ever finished the course. Only about half of eligible students earned primary school certificates; even fewer went on to complete secondary school. This means, Dubet says, that in the last years of the nineteenth century and well into the twentieth, the assimilation of many migrants, as of most workers, was effected in the workplace, not in the school. Those who did attend school were treated only as students, that is, as potentially reasonable individuals whose training took neither their social origins nor their emotional well-being into account. (American friends of mine, on sabbatical for a year in Paris in the early 1960s, encountered this ethos when they asked to meet with their daughter's teacher because they were concerned about how she was adjusting to her new environment. The teacher's brief reply startled them: "she is very well-behaved and her notebook is neat." So much for the psychologizing they were used to at parent-teacher conferences back home!) The teacher was there simply to promote learning, not to provide any other social services, and whatever there was of a youth culture at that time was to be left at the door of the school. For this reason the school was, in principle, a welcome place for children of minorities, such as Jews and Protestants. Teasing, racial epithets, and other forms of intolerance were not acceptable in this formal learning environment, although they undoubtedly occurred outside the doors of the classroom. Children wore regulation clothing or uniforms, and the sexes were taught separately; opposition to coeducation, Dubet explains, came from a desire to exclude social activities and emotions; "the largest part of moral education was left to families."[19] The mixed-sex schools that defenders of the headscarf ban now tout as the hallmark of laïcité—one of the signs of the republic's eternal commitment to gender equality—did not come into existence until the 1960s, and then only because shortages of funds for new construction mandated the end of separate buildings for boys and girls.

Changes began in the 1960s, but it was not until the 1970s that everyone expected to attend collège (our middle school) and even lycée (our high school). Dubet estimates that about half of any age cohort under twenty now attends school, many of them already earning wages even though they are still students. One measure of the expansion is overcrowding in classes. The proportion of overcrowded lycée classes, for example, rose from 9.4 percent in 1983 to 32.9 percent in 1990.[20] As school populations expanded, national education as a proportion of the state budget fell. In this context, social divisions between schools became more pronounced. For middle- and upper-class parents who knew how to work the system, placing one's child in a good school became a primary concern. Working-class parents had less social capital and less clout, so their children often ended up in poorer-quality schools, while children of families in the "immigrant" suburbs were confined to whatever was available in their neighborhoods. Needless to say, in these schools especially, social problems could not be left at the door. Paradoxically, as schools became an increasingly important avenue of upward mobility, attendance at some of them (those in ZEPs, a designation for trouble spots in the system that needed special attention and special funding) did not fulfill their promise, and this only increased the resentment of students for whom school attendance was a prerequisite for a job. During the riots in the fall of 2005, many students from the *banlieues* complained that their school attendance had not only been useless but harmful, because through it they were identified as coming from inferior places and so assumed to be ill-prepared for any job. Schools were not a means of integration but a way of reproducing, indeed guaranteeing, existing social hierarchies.

The massification of schooling was accompanied, Dubet tells us, by a new culture which brought the world of adolescence into the classroom. "Republican laïcité rested on a distance between school and society, but then the school gradually allowed itself to be swept up in a mass youth culture which it barely resisted."[21] In the aftermath of 1968, to the delight of many ardent secularists on the left, formal dress requirements were abandoned and there was new emphasis on the development of the whole child. The school became a place where individuality was encouraged (even as republican values were being taught), and students were granted the right to express themselves, to define their identities through distinctive clothing and hairstyles. "[F]or adolescents the 'look' is not simply an outer covering, but a true image of oneself, a face in the strong sense of the word."[22] In this context, where jeans and rasta hairdos were acceptable, many students (who themselves did not wear them) saw headscarves as another form of self-expression. So did some members of the clergy. "Don't confuse the problem of Islam with that of adolescence," Cardinal Lustiger warned proponents of the law.[23] But that was exactly what the law did, ignoring or denying the fact that the laïcité of the nineteenth and early twentieth centuries had long vanished, making the banning of headscarves an exception to the tolerant indulgence otherwise granted student expressions of identity. Several elder statesmen—first-rate social scientists, themselves the products of the schools of the first half of the twentieth century—insisted to me in conversation that the headscarf ban would somehow protect or restore the laïcité they had known and loved, as if no history had intervened between the 1930s and the present! Why would these supporters of the law, otherwise intelligent analysts of French institutions, somehow blame Muslims for the loss of the schools their memories cherished, a loss that had little or nothing to do with Islam? Their irrational insistence on the urgent need for a ban points up how overdetermined the headscarf was as a symbol of social and political disturbance.

Another moment of disciplinary action against an article of clothing complicated the headscarf debate, in both amusing and revealing ways. This was the "affaire du string." In October 2003, teachers and principals at some schools began sending home girls who were thought to be inadequately dressed because they were wearing "le string" (a thong), visible at the waistline of their low-cut pants and cropped tee shirts. This kind of outfit exceeded the bounds of acceptable self-expression, the teachers argued, turning classroom attention to matters erotic instead of intellectual. Some commentators linked the string and the veil as opposite sides of the same coin. In one case, the body was overexposed; in the other, it was too hidden. Girls wore the string to make themselves sexually attractive to boys; they wore the veil to refuse that possibility. For some feminists, the same subordination of women was at work in both cases; for others, there was a vast difference between the overt acknowledgment of desire and its suppression. When a government official proposed a return to uniforms as a way of getting rid of all these differences, his suggestion was opposed, on the one hand, by those who damned it as archaic and, on the other, by those who championed the right of young girls to follow the fashion of the day. Government intervention, from either point of view, was unacceptable. Needless to say, while the string was considered a fashion statement and little else (there was, of course, critical discussion of the pressures girls felt to follow fashion), the veil was taken to be far more dangerous, requiring a law to protect the republic from its influences. Many of those who bemoaned the self-exploitation girls were willing to undergo in pursuit of attention from boys were nevertheless unwilling to propose legal action to stop it; they acknowledged that the world of adolescence presented challenges of this kind and that it was the business of the school to work with that world and not to oppose it. These same people, however, thought that legal action to ban headscarves was necessary; *that* article of clothing was not about adolescent self-expression, or if it was, the form of self it was expressing was not an acceptable one.

The new emphasis on student self-expression, on the school's need to attend to the development of whole individuals, inevitably brought a change in teachers' roles: they were to be counselors, not just instructors. In theory, they were to be more sympathetic to the emotional demands of adolescence, closer to the lives and developmental issues of their students than their nineteenth-century counterparts had been. This may have worked well in primary schools and in collèges and lycées where students and teachers came from similar social milieux, but in poorer districts—the ZEPs—there was greater distance between teachers and students. (These schools make up about 10 percent of the total number nationally.) In these schools, students were faced with teachers who often did not understand or empathize with their situation, while the teachers confronted discipline problems that their predecessors or colleagues who taught in more elite districts had rarely seen. Facing challenges to their authority from angry, disaffected students and their parents, they not only felt a loss of control but found their professional identities destabilized. They no longer had the authority and the standing in the community that had once accrued to French schoolteachers. Add to this cuts in government funding for education, depressed salaries, and decreased spending for social services and community centers in the banlieues, and the difficulties for teachers were compounded.

It wasn't just discipline that was at issue, although that surely was a problem. The philosopher Etienne Balibar points out that the very status of knowledge has changed, the belief, once unquestioned, in the power of learning to shape people's minds and so their lives. It wasn't only that the instrumental notion of education, as the sure route to a good job, was belied by high rates of unemployment among "immigrant" youth, it was also—less tangibly, but no less certainly—that the concept of knowledge as a good thing in itself no longer carried the same weight in the culture as a whole. The power that came with knowledge once animated the desire for it and therefore excited both teachers and students. When that power was diminished, the reverence teachers could once anticipate simply because they *knew* so much declined; they were increasingly considered just another kind of state functionary, disciplinarians in the sense of rule enforcers instead of mind trainers.

Balibar argues that most teachers, even those not working in ZEPs, identified with the loss of status and authority so evident among their colleagues in those areas. For this reason, even though most of their members did not face the difficulties of those in the ZEPs, the major unions of secondary school teachers in France supported the ban on headscarves, and they were a powerful political constituency. They did this, Balibar suggests, because "they saw no other remedy for their impotence except the symbolic affirmation [of their authority] by the power of the state for which they worked. . . . Laïcité, whatever its definition, was not the end but the instrument of this corporate reflex."[24] Banning the headscarf seemed a strong gesture affirming the importance both of the school and the state, as well as of the intertwined relationship between them. Here once again we see how overdetermined was the symbolism of the veil. The fate of teachers was equated with that of the nation, and the line drawn at the headscarf was meant to secure them both. Instead of exploring the role the school could play in the new conditions of the twenty-first century, instead of asking on what (new or different) grounds the authority of teachers might be restored, the decision to ban headscarves placed the blame outside the system itself. The crisis in the schools—and indeed, there was one—was attributed to foreign influences, to "immigrants" whose values clashed with those of the republic. The solution was to eliminate the foreign influences and then everything would be all right—a delusional "fix" given the much larger set of social problems that needed to be addressed.

The Nation

When President Jacques Chirac created the Stasi commission in July 2003, he did so in the name of national unity. "France is a secular [*laïque*] republic," he wrote in his charge to Bernard Stasi. Since the law of 1905 separating church and state, laïcité has established "deep roots in our institutions." Indeed, that law had become a key aspect of "national cohesion," a way of guaranteeing that social differences would not fracture the unity of the nation. But the way of achieving unity involved denying the existence of the differences altogether. "The Republic is com-

posed of citizens," Chirac went on, "it must not be segmented
into groups." The "risk of a drift into communalism" must be
avoided. Nothing less than the future of the nation was at stake.
Already in 1989, the future of the nation was linked by many
commentators to what happened in the schools. Wrote one,
"The secular public school, the only appropriate expression of
the secular and republican community which is our nation, is in
danger. Today a headscarf, and tomorrow?"[25] The National Assembly committee's call in 2003 for a law banning headscarves
in public schools was an answer to that question. "More than
ever, the authorities must be vigilant about [enforcing] strict respect for the principle of laïcité."[26]

It is hard to imagine that a few schoolgirls wearing headscarves could bring down the nation or even produce fractures
in its foundation. But that was how the argument went. Not
only the president of the republic and most members of the
Stasi commission, but many politicians, journalists, and public
commentators, too, waxed apocalyptic on the issue of the
headscarf and the future of France. It was as if the headscarf
were the flag of an alien nation whose forces were intent on
compromising national integrity. These forces sought, it was
imagined, to corrupt the minds of the young and vulnerable
(represented most poignantly by schoolgirls), thereby eroding
laïcité, one of the pillars of the republic.

The headscarf law was informed by a particularly defensive
nationalism, one which rested on belief in the unchanging, indeed unchangeable, truth of a certain national identity. To
challenge that truth was to challenge the very idea of French
sovereignty and of the sovereign people whose will was said to
be incarnated in the national representation. Elsewhere I have

written on the way in which this vision of the nation rests on abstraction, on the idea of an abstract individual shorn of his social, religious, and ethnic identities.[27] Articulated at the time of the French Revolution as an alternative to the corporatist theories of the Old Regime, abstract individualism was the basis for citizenship and for the distinctively French concept of universalism. This universalism rested on an opposition between the political and the social, the abstract and the concrete. In the realm of the political, everyone was an individual—except for those whose lack of autonomy (initially women, slaves, and wage earners) made them unable to represent themselves. The claims of any group membership (this came under the rubric of "the social") must be shed if one were to be considered an individual. It was for this reason that, at the time of the revolution, Jews were initially excluded from citizenship. When they were enfranchised, it was as individuals, not as members of "a nation." There were some, however, who could never be dissociated from the group to which they belonged, who could therefore never become individuals. This was the case for women, whose sex was thought to make them incapable of abstraction (unlike men, they could not be detached from their bodies). As a concrete result, they did not receive the right to vote until 1945. For different reasons, Muslims are now in a similar position. Of course, they do qualify for formal citizenship, but their membership in a religious community that does not conceive of individuals as able to categorize their beliefs in terms of public or private makes them not susceptible to abstraction, hence incapable of assimilation.

Since the 1980s and especially since the celebrations of the bicentennial of the revolution in 1989, there has been increasing emphasis on the idea of the unity and indivisibility of the nation. This emphasis has acquired mythological status, obscuring the long and complicated history of various group struggles for rights in France, the most obvious being the successful campaigns of workers for recognition of the reality of class divisions in the social body. And though abstraction is the principle of universalism, in practice it is sameness, achieved through cultural assimilation, that guarantees national unity. Individuals must not only be autonomous, they must also share what are thought to be eternal French values in order to be taken seriously. For this reason, current demands for social and legal recognition by various groups—women, homosexuals, and "immigrants"—have been met with denunciation: they are communalist, they give priority to group membership, they introduce "unnatural" differences that will rend the social fabric and weaken the body of the nation.

The excuse (in the name of unity) of protecting the nation from the demands of some of its citizens has been used to block action on behalf of groups underserved by the generous (for some) provisions of the French welfare state. American affirmative action is anathema in France, not for the same reasons that right-wingers here have objected to it (because it applies tests other than individual merit to those whose paths have long been blocked by discrimination), but because it is contrary to French universalism and to the national unity that it necessarily creates. From this perspective, discrimination does not exist, because differences of groups are not recognized; if differences don't exist, how can there be discrimination?

The unacceptable demands of domestic groups have been attributed to external pressures—from the European Union and other international institutions like the United Nations—that in themselves undermine national sovereignty by substituting rules from elsewhere for those that are French. The historian Timothy Smith argues that blaming outside pressures is a way for French elites to refuse to address the internal problems that need attention: high unemployment rates; grossly unequal employment and pay rates for youth, women, and "immigrants" as compared to previous generations; a health care and pension system that protects older, entrenched, public-sector employees at the expense of the young and the poor. These are not, he says, the result of "globalization"—often cited as an inescapable, uncontrollable force undermining national sovereignty—but of domestic political decision-making that opts to protect the established classes (some 60 percent of the population) at the expense of its marginalized others. These days, he argues, French politicians displace blame elsewhere rather than taking responsibility themselves.

Although I think he underestimates the impact of Europeanization and globalization, I find Smith's analysis helpful for explaining the way in which the law against headscarves was depicted as a defense of the republic. The discussion of headscarves, couched in extreme nationalist rhetoric, shifted the conversation away from the problems posed by a large, impoverished population—many of whom have lived for decades as citizens in France, many of whom are non-practicing Muslims or more culturally than religiously identified as such, and are certainly not political radicals—to an imaginary threat posed by Islam. This is not to deny that there are terrorists on French soil; it is to say, however, that there is a far more momentous question facing French decision-makers: how to achieve the integration of former colonial subjects as "fully French" into a society of which they have already long been a part.

It is hard not to agree with the anthropologist Emmanuel Terray when he argues that the headscarf controversy was a form of "political hysteria" in which real social anxieties were displaced onto phantasmatic enemies and phantasmatic solutions were offered in place of concrete social policy.[28] The problem of the status of immigrants and of the racist practices that kept them on the margins of French society was redefined as a problem of Islamism, an external threat with links to Iran and Saudi Arabia. The solution was an endorsement of militant secularism as a counterweight—a secularism conceived as the truth of French national identity rather than as the ground on which such identity could be negotiated. That went along with a defensive insistence on preserving the homogeneity of the nation in the face of evidence that France's populace was socially divided. In defiance of this evidence, social divisions were blamed on the stubborn refusal of Muslims to integrate, on the inherent "foreignness" of their "culture." It followed that the cure for discrimination was the denial that differences existed at all; if they did, it was the fault of "communalism"—a concept alien to France.

There was, of course, a crisis, but not the one proponents of the law diagnosed. Instead, the elevation of laïcité as the unquestioned and immutable truth of French republicanism was the symptom of a set of difficult problems: how to improve the lot of an impoverished, marginalized "immigrant" population, and, more generally, how to recognize difference in social *and* political terms. Instead of confronting these problems head-on, the leaders of politics and opinion (with a few exceptions) resorted to a kind of knee-jerk racism that demonstrated the paucity of their philosophical resources and the weakness of their political capacities.

Conclusion

It would be a mistake to conclude, as some of the proponents of the headscarf ban argued, that the version of secularism they endorsed was the only version possible. Harking back to 1789, they insisted, against good historical evidence to the contrary, that the integrity of the republic rested on a firm refusal of religion in the schools and in the state. This was dubbed the "republican model" of laïcité. In fact, as Jean Baubérot (the lone dissenting member of the Stasi commission and a historian of laïcité) has pointed out, the idea of laïcité has had a long history in France, and some of its definitions are very much at odds with the definition offered in the heat of the headscarf controversy. There is at least one other "model" of laïcité, a "democratic model," that some diehards dismiss as "Anglo-American" and hence foreign to France, but that Baubérot places squarely within a French context (thus demonstrating that there is more than one version of the story of laïcité). Between 1985 and 1990, he writes, the League of Education, a confederation of societies of teachers and others interested in education, offered a far-reaching plan. The left was in power at this point, and was more open than it would later become to thinking about how to address issues of difference that were plaguing domestic politics. Baubérot writes that the league first revisited the founding texts of the doctrine, insisting on laïcité as the "conscience of democracy," an effort to "prevent the ossi-

fication of scientific thought into dogma," and "to contain religion within its limits without denying its immense cultural
significance."[29]

In the League's proposals, which looked toward the year
2000, laïcité was a ground on which difficult problems could be
assessed:

> Take for example . . . the conflict which, among "chil-
> dren of immigrants," opposes the culture taught at school
> and that handed down by the family. . . . In this situation,
> to ensure "rights to the languages of emigration is a duty
> of laïcité," and a "bilingual education" must be promoted
> in which "the thorough knowledge of the mother lan-
> guage as the basis of the identity of an historic commu-
> nity" is added to the "knowledge of a language of world
> communication which enables full participation in uni-
> versal dialogue." Moreover, it is necessary to abandon a
> concept of the universal centered on Western values and
> to recognize "the universal aspect contained in various
> particular cultures." French messianism, which considers
> this country to be the bearer of universal values . . . is cer-
> tainly a precious heritage, but to be progressively rejuve-
> nated it must become a French contribution toward the
> elaboration of a new universality, the outcome of an en-
> counter of cultures and values.

The school was the place where children would engage in the
kind of "reflection, criticism, [and] experimentation" that was
the hallmark of democracy. The greatest dangers to the
achievement of this democracy were seen to come from "'civil
clerics': abusive experts, a large state corps imbued with privi-

leges, bosses by divine right, arrogant senior officials invested in their views as the only truth. The laïcité of the year 2000 must ensure that the citizens are not deprived of public debates on essential questions relating to medical ethics, information, education, etc."[30] In this vision the school is indeed a cradle of democracy, in which differences are mediated and negotiated, established practices are critically revisited and revised, and debate is allowed to flourish in the absence of dogmatic assertions of immutable truth. In that sense, it is a preparation for citizenship, for participation in the work of a nation conceptualized as a heterogeneous entity, in which the differences of its constituents are understood to be a resource, not a deficiency.

Baubérot concludes by suggesting that historically the two models of secularism have long been in tension in France, that the democratic model has already been applied to Christians and Jews and that it "would be disastrous if we were to apply the republican model effectively only to Islam."[31] It is the democratic model, he believes, that "constitutes an opportunity for a future in which sociocultural and socioreligious conflicts have been relatively mastered and contribute to the construction of the future." For Baubérot it is not religion but the republican model that, by taking the religious and the secular to be absolute opposites, poses the most dangerous obstacle to democracy.

4

INDIVIDUALISM

As the headscarf controversy raged, the question of the intention of its wearers nagged at those who claimed they already knew what it was. What did this "conspicuous" display of religious affiliation signify? Why did girls wear veils? Were they freely chosen or forced upon them? Could the headscarf be considered a legitimate expression of individual conscience and therefore warrant protection under liberal secular law? The answers varied, but the voices of the girls themselves were strikingly absent from the debates. The Stasi commission interviewed only a few girls who wore headscarves and then in private session, away from audiences that might have been swayed by what they said. In any case, the commission paid little heed to their accounts. Only after the law was passed did a few books appear which gave firsthand testimony, but, coming after the fact, these were unable to influence the legislative proceedings. Even if they had appeared earlier, they probably would have had little effect because the arguments they advanced were heard as an endorsement of an Islam incompatible either with any other religion or with secularism.

Those supporting the ban, as well as many of those who opposed it, believed, in accordance with laïcité, that religion should be one of a number of values an individual espoused; it was a private matter that must be readily separated from one's public life. Individuals were autonomous, in this view, with no obligations other than to themselves; their choices did not define them but were expressions of the rational beings they already were. The abstract individual, in other words, must be realized in fact. The idea that there might be what political philosopher Michael Sandel calls "'encumbered selves' claimed by duties they cannot renounce, even in the face of civil obligations that may conflict" was not part of the definition of the individual in this French republican discourse.[1] Unless individuals could be divided between public (secular) commitments and private (religious) ones, they did not qualify for membership in the republic. When some of the girls wearing headscarves insisted that they could not do otherwise because "the headscarf is part of myself"[2]—that is, there was no separation between a self and its religious embodiment—their critics replied that this was ridiculous: either they were delusional (overcome by irrational sentiments), dishonest (acting as agents of political Islam), or, most likely, forced by (male) family members into acts they would otherwise refuse. From this perspective, wearing the veil did not represent a choice that could be respected as such.

Those who supported the ban conceived of it as a valiant action by the modern French state to rescue girls from the obscurity and oppression of traditional communities, thus opening their lives to knowledge and freedom, even if it meant expelling them from school. The contradiction—that legislation designed to provide choice ended up by denying it—was not perceived as such by the law's champions. This was because of their faith in the superiority of their philosophy, their equation of it with universalism, progress, and civilization. To justify imposing a law on these young women, the proponents of the ban had to identify them as victims who had been denied the right to choose by an oppressive, authoritarian community.

Ironically, many of the girls who donned headscarves defined their action as a personal choice, one made in the face of parental disapproval and as part of an individual search for the spiritual values they found lacking in their communities and the society at large. It seems to me that Olivier Roy is right to link this rediscovery of Islam by younger generations of Muslims in the West to other forms of contemporary religious revivalism (born-again Christianity, charismatic Catholicism, orthodox Judaism) and to New Age religions more generally. Here is how he describes the phenomenon:

> The stress in religiosity is upon . . . the importance of self-achievement, attempts to reconstruct a religious community based on the individual commitment of the believer in a secular environment (hence the blossoming of sects), a personal quest for an immediately accessible knowledge in defiance of the established religious authority, the juxtaposition of a fundamentalist approach to the law (to obey God in every facet of one's daily life) with syncretism and spiritual nomadism, the success of gurus and self-appointed religious leaders, and so on.[3]

In Roy's view, this kind of religiosity among Muslims is already a sign of their modernity and of their adoption of the values of Western individualism, whether or not they define their practice as the subordination of the self to God. Even if Roy's analysis accounts for the motives of only some of the wearers of headscarves, his insistence that we take the phenomenon to be "modern" is crucial for my argument.

The French who argued for a law against headscarves defined contemporary Islamic religiosity as a return to traditional Islam, essentially theocratic in its aspirations. It was therefore unlike any other religion confronting this secular state. Until the ban on headscarves, yarmulkes and Sikh turbans had been permitted in French classrooms. It was Islam that provoked the call for restriction—Islam defined as a singular culture, at once politically dangerous and personally oppressive. In the legislators' construction of it, the girls in headscarves were captives in a culture that held them against their will; it was the responsibility of the state to set them free.

As I have been suggesting, the opposition between French and Islamic cultures was an ideological construction that reduced complex realities to simple, oppositional categories. On the question of choice, the opposition was between individual autonomy and cultural compulsion. The basis for French republican theory is the autonomous individual who exists prior to his or her choices of lifestyle, values, and politics; these are but external expressions of a fixed inner self, a self which by definition cannot relinquish its autonomy. Critics of this theory point out that the individual is not entirely autonomous, because s/he operates within a set of normative parameters that define individuality (and Frenchness) and that rule out other options. French citizens are "encumbered" just as religious subjects are, according to these critics, for they understand themselves in terms they did not choose; the notion of the individual as existing prior to external influence masks its status as a cultural belief.

The other side of the opposition (Islam = cultural compulsion) has also been criticized by those who point out that Islam is not alone in its religious or spiritual constructions of "encumbered" personhood. It shares with other religions the subordination of the self to divine authority and its commands. If the sharp division between public and private, religion and the state, had its origins historically in Christianity (and especially Protestantism), New Age religiosity, Roy suggests, understands the self to be indivisible; private and public are not meaningful moral or ethical distinctions. Although there are still important differences among various religiosities, they share the idea that the self is not constituted by its own authority but by religious norms. These norms prescribe a series of ethical practices for the realization of a self, what the anthropologist Saba Mahmood, when describing Islam, calls "habituated learning." There is no distinction between inner and outer, she says; rather, "the outward behavior of the body constitutes both the potentiality, and the means, through which an interiority is realized."[4] For some women, the veil is "a means both of being and becoming a certain kind of person," one who is moral and virtuous, according to their readings of the Koran. (The same can be said, in reference to their own scriptures, of Jewish men wearing yarmulkes, Jewish women putting on wigs, and Sikh men wrapping their hair in turbans.) This person, anthropologist Talal Asad tells us (again referring to Islam), is an individual who is "self-governing but not autonomous. The *shari'a*, a system of practical reason morally binding on each faithful individual, exists independently of him or her. At the same time, every Muslim has the psychological ability to discover its rules and to conform to them."[5]

That at least some Muslim girls were embarked on such a path of discovery and that their path had something in common with other denominational religiosities could not be entertained by those debating the law. That individualism might also be a form of faith was equally unacceptable. For those who urged a ban on headscarves, the autonomous self was an objective fact. Those supporting the law understood the issue to be a confrontation between Islamic culture and French individualism. The headscarf could only be an imposition of that culture; its removal a sign that liberty and equality had prevailed.

The Arguments for the Law

In the reports of the two investigative bodies appointed to look into the issue of headscarves in public schools, the veil was presented either as a denial of freedom or a loss of reason. "Objectively," Bernard Stasi concluded, "the veil stands for the alienation of women."[6] But even in the most eloquent justifications for the law there was a contradiction: a decision to wear the veil could never be seen as reasonable choice. While admitting that a few (*certains*) girls considered the veil a means of emancipation, the National Assembly study group insisted that many more (*beaucoup*) felt it oppressive.[7] There were, needless to say, no statistics offered to back up this assertion, just anecdotes and the opinions of "experts" who already agreed that a law banning headscarves was needed. It was not so much a desire to misrepresent the facts that prevented a systematic study as it was the strongly held belief that free individuals would never willingly choose the veil.

The primary conclusion of both committees was that young girls, with no ability to resist the pressure, had been forced by their fathers or, more often, their brothers and other young men in the community to publicly proclaim their subordination. There was only one meaning for the veil, sociologist Juliette Minces told the National Assembly committee: it stood for Islam's belief that women were inferior, sexually dangerous, and in need of protection.[8] Without the veil, girls were assumed by the men around them to be "loose women," dishonoring their families and therefore open to the punishments of harassment, beating, and even gang rape—(such were the images offered of the reign of terror in the banlieues). While there is no question that aggression by boys against girls was a real fact of life in these neighborhoods (as it was in other, nonimmigrant neighborhoods), the situation was exaggerated by the lawmakers. The oversexed Arab boy or man is an old racist stereotype (see chapter 2), and it was used to great effect during the headscarf controversy. These men's violence was supposed to be legitimated by Islamic teaching: girls without headscarves were fair game for sexual assault. One girl, who insisted that it was her choice alone to wear a headscarf, wondered how banning it would solve the problem she acknowledged these boys sometimes posed—shouldn't the *boys* be punished for their misbehavior? The legislators' reply was that the state would protect minor females, who were, by definition, unable to protect themselves; it would choose the true path of emancipation for them. (In effect, responsibility was being passed from one set of fathers to another.) State power would overwhelm those who forced girls to behave in what one witness called an "unnatural" way. The law asserted the primacy of the nation over communal customs and practices. "There are pressures constraining young girls to wear religious signs. Their family and social environment impose on them a choice that is not their own. The Republic cannot remain deaf to these girls' cry of distress. The space of the school must remain for them a place of liberty and emancipation; it must not become a place of suffering and humiliation."[9] In the reasoning of one of the commission members, sociologist Patrick Weil, a law would not only protect girls who didn't want to wear headscarves from social pressure but would enable girls who did wear them to make the choice they really wanted to make anyway, the choice never to wear a headscarf.[10] Although there was evidence to the contrary—that many girls had donned the headscarf on their own initiative, indeed against the wishes of their parents—the commission members could not accept this as an exercise of free choice. Moreover, they saw the action of those girls who did wear headscarves as a potential, if not actual, infringement on the free will of girls who didn't want to wear them. It was finally the individuality of the latter girls—those who had made the right choice—that the state had to protect, even if that meant preventing a small minority from doing what they chose.

Anyway, if there were girls who had freely chosen headscarves, supporters of the ban were sure it was for the wrong reasons. Since veils were seen to be the emblem of an international Islamist movement reaching to France from Pakistan, Iran, and Saudi Arabia, girls who wore them, perhaps without knowing it, were declaring allegiance to foreign powers. Or

perhaps they did know it; how was one to tell? In the imagination of supporters of the ban, the veil itself signified a deliberate confusion of meaning; its purpose was to dissimulate, never
to disclose. So a good student, who attended all classes and received high grades, might really be a rebel; her commitments
political, not at all religious. And how to differentiate between
religious and political in what was, after all, an ideological
struggle pitting East against West? Since expert after expert
testified that there was no obligation under Koranic law to
wear a veil, it could only be the influence of "fundamentalists"
with devious political motives that was in evidence. Moreover,
how determine the effect on their more secular-leaning class-
mates of some students wearing headscarves? Was it a rebuke?
A call to conscience? A threat? "It's difficult to draw a line between what is ostentatious and a protest—an act of proselytizing forbidden by law—and the 'normal' wearing of signs of religious conviction," the National Assembly report warned.[11] It
might be possible for teachers to know the difference, but
judges and legislators were not in a position to discern it. And
it was they who were charged with establishing and enforcing
national norms.

The confusion of meanings was intolerable to those for
whom transparency was a mark not only of modernity but of
moral rectitude. Although headscarves were the issue—only
the hair, ears, and neck were covered—they were usually referred to as veils, enhancing the sense of a cover-up. Veils allowed for great play in fantasies of invisibility and visibility,
darkness and light, blindness and full sightedness. The veil is a
"curtain," said psychoanalyst Elisabeth Roudinesco. It shrouds
a young girl in silence.[12] She is made both blind and deaf, los-

ing the senses that connect her to the world. It denies her access, added philosopher Alain Finkielkraut, to the great works of culture, preventing her from developing her rational faculties literally keeping her in the dark.[13] It was a veil of ignorance that could not be penetrated by critical thought. Girls were forced to wear them against their will: a veil is a rape ("un voile est un viol") testified one feminist of North African origin.[14] The girls were victims, but they were also threats. Veils were, after all, masks. "Some of our Belgian friends, parodying Magritte, have told us 'it's only a veil,'" reported Jacqueline Costa-Lascoux, a member of the Stasi commission. "But the veil has served as a mask for all those who want to hide themselves."[15] Masks were dangerous because they allowed for misrepresentations of the truth of the wearer; they were the ruse of imposters. It was sometimes unclear who the imposters were, men themselves disguised in veils, or men forcing girls to wear them to accomplish nefarious deeds, or the girls themselves. A television interviewer asked Jacques Chirac during his 1994 campaign for the presidency whether he thought the veil *affaire* was a "screen—if one can call it that—for other desires of Islamist movements?" Chirac replied that it was certainly "a provocation."[16] In this same period, *Le Figaro* ran a headline that read: "The hidden face of the headscarf controversy: what's under the veil." The accompanying story told of terrorist links between French Islamists and Saudi Arabia.[17] More than one proponent of the law warned, ominously, that the veil was political Islam's Trojan horse: "A veil can hide a beard."[18] In their excesses of meaning and confusion of boundaries, veils were literally instruments of terror.

The only solution—the only way to achieve transparency—

was to strip away the offending tissue by passage of a law that
was "brief, simple, clear, subject to as little interpretation as
possible."[19] The president of the National Assembly's study
group maintained that "The prohibition of the wearing of 'visible' religious and political signs in schools means not only the
prohibition of 'ostentatious' signs, whose limits have been very
difficult to establish, but of all signs that the eye can see [tout
signe que l'oeil peut voir]."[20] His suggestion was rejected, but it
was agreed that the law must provide an objective measure to
eliminate all distinctive signs. That other signs were swept
along with it in the interests of equal treatment—skullcaps and
large crosses—was beside the point. The target was the veil
and the obfuscation it permitted. This became clear when "discreet" signs (presumably not so small that the eye could not see
them)—medallions, small crosses, hands of Fatima, Korans,
and stars of David—were permitted. Since literally nothing
could be hidden behind them, they were considered innocuous
and thus permissible expressions of private conviction.

When it came to head coverings, the law refused all compromises; it would not permit bandanas or headbands or small
scarves, as mediators had previously agreed to in particular
cases. These were thought to muddy the issue, since they
granted the validity of the *desire* to wear a veil, even if the particular head covering was only a gesture, and incomplete at
that. The desire itself was taken to be illegitimate since it was
constrained or deceptive or subversive, a gesture of community
attachment at odds with the independent nature of individuals.
Autonomous individuals might hold religious beliefs, but these
must be separable from their sense of self; privatized belief (invisible or discreet) would not compromise their independence.

Beyond the equation of veils with terrorism was the refusal to acknowledge that, for some of these girls at least, there was a different notion of personhood being articulated, one they had chosen themselves. In the end the law insisted that only one notion was possible—the unencumbered, autonomous individual; another model was inconceivable. Indeed, only such individuals were thought to be capable of exercising choice. Upon those individuals lay the entire structure of French republicanism—or so it was claimed. "What is in question is our very conception of the citizen. . . . France is not a union of different groups; it is a community of individuals free of their personal group attachments."[21] Banning headscarves in public schools made the point clearly that only one notion of personhood was possible if Muslims were to be accepted as fully French. In other words, one could not be both Muslim and French; assimilation was the only route to membership in the nation.

The Arguments against the Law

Opponents of prohibition rejected the equation of headscarves with radical Islamism, insisting instead that there were many motives for wearing them. Although their arguments rarely took the religious motives expressed by some of the girls at face value, they did insist that individual choice and not community pressure was the operative factor. Opponents of the ban sought to bring complexity into the debate, refusing the simple oppositions between Islam and France. They offered sociological explanations for the practice of wearing headscarves and insisted that it be seen in its historical and social contexts. They operated within the terms of republican discourse, while refusing the polarizing characterizations offered by supporters of the law. If individuals were making the wrong choice (opting against modernity and its emancipatory promise)—and even this was questionable—they were doing so for plausible reasons.

First among these reasons was a skepticism about democracy, born of its association with French colonial rule. The veil, after all, had played an important role during the Algerian War as a sign of refusal of French domination. More recently—and in what for many was simply a postcolonial continuation of that same rule—the French government had supported the authoritarian secularist regime in Algeria when it canceled the elections that probably would have brought an Islamist majority to power. From this perspective, endorsing Islam was a way of commenting on the hypocrisy of the proponents of democratic secularism, and of embracing something that claimed to be an incorrupt alternative to it. Islam, some sociologists who opposed the law insisted, was a site of resistance to secular modernity, a place where young people from immigrant families, living in poverty in the metropole, could find the orientation and structure that was absent in modern cities. This structure might once have been provided by left-wing organizations such as trade unions, the Communist Party, and various other militant political associations. These once had helped to integrate youth into French society by identifying them as members of a class struggling for its emancipation. But such organizations no longer performed their integrating functions (some were frankly hostile to Arabs), and so Muslim institutions—mosques, philanthropic societies, social welfare programs, and neighborhood cultural centers—had taken their place.

Still, no single Muslim identity emanated from these institutions, sociologists cautioned, and so the headscarf was a sign with many meanings. While supporters of the law worked hard to reduce those many meanings to one, those who opposed it insisted that the complexity be acknowledged. Françoise Gaspard and Fharad Khosrokhavar concluded, after extensive interviews during 1994 with girls wearing them, that the headscarf had at least three meanings. As worn by immigrant women, it was a tie to the world from which they had come, a nostalgic hold on a fading tradition. Another was the one worn by adolescents whose families demanded it as a sign of modesty, a way of controlling sexuality. This was a reworking of tradition, a way of dealing with the chaos of urban life, and it allowed girls from orthodox families to gain access to public places—schools, for example, or jobsites—otherwise forbidden them. A third was the scarf chosen by young women as a form of self-protection, or as an expression of identity—a way they found to assert themselves in environments that endangered and discriminated against them. The headscarf gave them a dignity they were otherwise denied. Whether on the streets of their neighborhoods or in the eyes of French society, it was a way of talking back.

The headscarf conferred an Islamic identity on its wearer, but Khosrokhavar and others insisted that the identity differed according to social standing—in fact, there were even more than the three meanings he and Gaspard had identified. For young people from impoverished immigrant communities, Islam seemed to offer a way out of the demeaning circumstances of a compromised French nationality. It could be a means of refusing both parental discipline and social pressure. Here was an imagined international community to which they could aspire, one which rewarded their discipline and purity and which aligned them with what seemed revolutionary forces, resisting the corruptions of secular, Western capitalism. For those from more integrated, better-off families, who were spared the difficulties of life in the banlieues but who nonetheless faced regular discrimination in their chosen fields, Islam was a way of demanding respect for difference, a call for integration without assimilation. Green Party leader Alain Lipietz suggested that the message of the scarf was anti-assimilationist, but not anti-French. It was as Franco-Muslims that the girls wanted to be accepted.[22] Educator and jurist Dounia Bouzar offered an additional comment on the way Islam could function to promote integration. "By 'returning to Islam' the young person henceforth belongs to. . . a community of believers throughout the world," she wrote. Adhering to a strictly religious criterion of identity, one which is by definition extranational, allows what she referred to as the "de-ethnicization" of believers: "there is no longer any need to be Algerian or Moroccan in order to be a Muslim. Paradoxically, the passage to Islam permits one to be considered French on French soil."[23]

The opponents of the law insisted on the Frenchness of the headscarf, its difference from a veil imposed by an Islamist state. In the French context, Khosrokhavar pointed out, the veil was not a choice forced by the state but rather the sign of a certain modernity. It was the expression of "the autonomy of newly urbanized youth of rural origin, or of young people from modest urban backgrounds . . . who demand social recognition by adhering to a code of modesty, honor, physical and cultural integrity different from that of the dominant secular classes."[24]

This desire for recognition was also a protest against discrimination, and this was taken to be a major motive for the religiosity of young French Muslims. Like the adoption of the word "nigger" by blacks in the United States, wearing a headscarf assumed the stigmatized object as a positive attribute. "When I was a kid at school," commented Nadia Zanoun, "I was ashamed of my name, I wanted to hide my Algerian origins. They [the young girls with hijabs], in contrast, have the courage I never had to affirm their Arabness. Their headscarves also testify to an immense desire for respect."[25] In the conflation of "Arabness" and Islam, the headscarf is taken as a reply to the continued experience of discrimination, to the failure of the universalist promise of French republicanism to fully include North Africans because they could not be abstracted from the marks of their difference.[26] The demand now was to recognize, not to suppress, that difference. The message of the headscarf, philosopher Charlotte Nordmann and publisher Jérôme Vidal said, might be a variation on the slogan of the American gay-rights group Act-Up: "We're here, we're from here, get used to it!"[27]

Far from representing the subordination of women, these gestures demonstrated a desire for, if not the actual achievement of, agency. Various commentators stressed the need to see the seemingly contradictory and productive import of the choices being made, the individual agency it permitted. The headscarf could be at once a concession to family pressure *and* a statement of individual autonomy even when it involved acceptance of Islamic codes of modesty. Paradoxically, girls in headscarves got to play a political role as embodiments of communal aspiration, even when politics was supposed to be off-limits for women, and even as their status as future mothers and wives was being affirmed. Wearing a headscarf might be a way of adhering to community rules *and* asserting pride in one's identity in the face of discrimination. It could also be a simple form of self-defense, a way of avoiding abuse at the hands of one's brothers or male neighbors, hence a way of escaping oppression rather than submitting to it. Here the opponents of the ban on headscarves found assertions of individual will that had little to do with real religious belief and that, under the guidance of teachers and republican principles, could be nurtured and eventually won over to more secular ways of thinking. Wasn't that, after all, the purpose of the republican school?

Whether the headscarf had been chosen or imposed, critics of the law argued that it was a mistake to ban its wearers from the schools of the nation. In an article published in *Libération* (May 20, 2003), three sociologists and two philosophers presented their case. They called on feminists, parents, students, and teachers to mobilize against the law. "In all cases, it is in welcoming them [girls in headscarves] to the secular school that we can help emancipate them, by giving them the means of achieving autonomy." If the girls weren't already free agents, they would become so at school; no religious attire could hinder the liberating effects of a French education. "In sending them away, we condemn them to oppression." Rhetorically, the five authors gestured to a *choice* to wear a headscarf; they might consider it an ill-advised choice, but the fact that it was a choice showed that some kind of autonomy was already at work. These girls were ripe for the emancipation that exposure to the best French values would inevitably bring about.

The Law's Targets

The girls wearing headscarves were rarely heard in the debates about the law, but when they were, some insisted that they had acted freely; identifying with Islam was not a constraint imposed by others but a choice they themselves had made. This choice could emanate from individual will, or it could be the kind of choice Asad describes as creating an individual who is "self-governing, but not autonomous." Here the self is produced, as Mahmood describes it, through a series of ethical practices whose authority emanates from divine command. It is not that one turns oneself over to God but that one cannot imagine existing apart from his rules. There is "cultivated" what Mahmood calls a specific "architecture of the self" that needs to be examined on its own terms.[28] It was this architecture that was entirely neglected in the debates about headscarves, and for that reason, I want to highlight it here.

It is important to note that in the following discussion I do not claim to be representing all headscarf-wearing girls. Like the critics of the ban I have already discussed in this chapter, I think there are many motives, not all of them consciously articulated, involved in the decision to put on a headscarf (the choice is as overdetermined as the one to ban headscarves). Still, the viewpoint of those who did offer religious motives for their action provides insight into an entirely silenced aspect of these *affaires*. The religious explanations offered also reveal the complexity of the issue: the girls at once invoked individualism in terms familiar to republican discourse and spiritual commitments that rest on a very different notion of individual choice.

Two books published in France in 2003 and 2004 provide important insight into the motivations of some of the girls who wore headscarves. The first, *Ordinary Girls* (*Des filles comme les autres*) is a set of interviews between two secular academics and the Lévy sisters, who were at the center of the 2003 controversy (see chapter 1). The second, *One Veiled, the Other*

Not (*Une voilée,* / *l'autre pas*), is an exchange between two French Muslim women. They, in turn, comment on testimonies gathered from other well-educated young women, most of whom have chosen to wear headscarves. The views of the authors are often starkly different, and they do not try to change each other's minds "but to understand what the other has to say with profound mutual respect." Both books "speak of headscarves without forgetting those who wear them" and insist that they are talking not about a foreign import but a "French phenomenon."[29] Girls in headscarves, as the title of the Lévy sisters' book proclaims, are girls like any others.

In these books, the girls and women who wear headscarves insist, first of all, that the decision to wear one was freely made, an aspect of a personal quest. No one forced them to do it; indeed, the choice often meant battles with family and friends. The second prominent theme was the search for faith and interior structure, a familiar refrain that I (following Roy) associate with religiosity. Finally, one notes the absence of references to family members or religious leaders who told them what to do; the girls' personal relationship to texts and the dogmatic application of their own interpretations is a striking feature of the accounts. The authority to accept religious prescription, paradoxically, lies in the willing self. The girls speak of a spiritual quest and a philosophy of life; of faith and the ways to enact it. It is clear that they think of themselves as having made a decision to take responsibility for their actions and beliefs. What they are after seems more often an abandonment of ego than an assertion of it; at the same time, the self is very much at the center of how they conceive of what they do. They appear to be striving for what Mahmood describes as a "concordance of inward motives, outward actions, inclinations, and emotional states through the repeated practice of virtuous deeds."[30] Primary among these deeds are prayer and the wearing of headscarves.

Saïda Kada, the veiled author of *One Veiled, the Other Not*, is the founder of French Muslim Women in Action (Femmes françaises et musulmanes engagées), an association devoted to improving the image of Muslim women by entering the arena of public debate about them—offering the voice that usually isn't heard. She describes her view of the place of the veil in the system of Islamic belief. A woman dons the veil, she says, not because the Koran requires it, but because it is one of the steps taken in the construction of one's spiritual relationships. "One is a Muslim first; one adheres to a certain philosophy of life and, in this context, one wants to wear the headscarf. The discovery of Islam is marked by a series of steps that successively fashion your identity by leading you to find an equilibrium in yourself, in God, and with others."[31] Kada's is the same trajectory that Alma Lévy describes for herself: "I began by praying. . . . In order to pray, you have to cover your head. Quickly, I found it impossible to put on the veil when I prayed and to take it off when I went outside. Undressing in order to go out seemed incongruous to me: the headscarf was a part of myself."[32] Interviewed outside a lycée in Lille, a girl in a headscarf spoke of wearing it as a way of "concretizing" her faith. Her best friend, standing beside her with her head uncovered, did not reject the headscarf; she simply wasn't yet ready, she said, to take that step.[33] Kada's comment elaborates this outlook: "You can't understand the headscarf without talking about the whole spiritual progression that goes with it. For a young girl the logic is not 'with or without the headscarf.' She begins to feel herself 'with' it in a progressive journey of faith, where she discovers things strongly linked to spirituality."[34] The anthropologist Abdellah Hammoudi talks about the effects of ritual in terms that may help explain these comments: "ritual transforms the subject by giving him or her a world to inhabit that is shifted away from the empirical, social, and pragmatic world—hence also shifted vis-à-vis the world of conscious or unconscious rationality. Not that it eliminates the latter; rather, it relates to them in concealments or displacements, thus coloring life and action."[35]

For some of the girls interviewed, a spiritual commitment involved submitting oneself not to men or man-made laws but to God. "Through knowledge of God my faith grew and I wanted to wear the veil as a sign of humility."[36] For others, spiritual commitment could lead to compromise on the visible, material level in order to satisfy God's will. When she understood that pursuing knowledge would bring her closer to God, Nassera decided to take off her headscarf, because her teachers constantly berated her for wearing it and all the legal proceedings had made it so controversial. "I thought about the headscarf: it represented only the materiality of the modesty that was already within me. I could continue to embody [that modesty] by wearing loose clothing. . . . Despite the discomfort it caused me, I took off my scarf." School, she reflected, contributed to her spiritual maturity, and it was her spirituality, she said, that pushed her to stay in school. She recounts her actions as entirely personal, individual decisions, based on her own interpretation of the Koran. "As soon as I finished the lycée, I covered my hair again. My headscarf had never really left me.

Beyond an identity, it's an accomplishment for me."[37] For Nassera, education was mandated by her religious beliefs, and it only served to intensify, not diminish, them. The opposition between religion and learning insisted on by supporters of the headscarf ban didn't seem to hold in this case.

And what of the subordination of women? Wasn't the veil always a symbol of that, as so many feminist supporters of the law charged? The responses to this question varied; indeed, it is their variety that needs to be taken into account. Houria talked about finding respect and dignity when she put on the hijab; her brothers, who before had harassed her, were no longer able to control her. Paradoxically, she had gained a certain emancipation through her submission. For Dounia Bouzar, who did not wear one, a headscarf meant accepting women's inequality with men. "It would mean admitting that I would never be considered equal, that that was what God wanted."[38] In contrast, for Saïda Kada, who did wear the headscarf, it signified submission only to God, not to men, the acceptance of women as individuals before their God. If some men had abused the teachings of the Koran in order to "sacralize their domination" of women, she argued, this was neither the only interpretation of Islamic teaching nor an acceptable one. And interpretation was, after all, the name of the game. The public debates about the law had focused on only the most sexist and archaic interpretations of women's position, Kada pointed out, and presented those as the essential—the only—meaning of it. But this misrepresentation confused rather than clarified the issue for Muslim women. "By imagining that our emancipation can come only by struggling against Islam and rejecting the veil, we flout the founding Muslim principle which consists of rereading the meaning of texts in relation to contemporary contexts. This gives us other choices than breaking with our religion in order to evolve."[39] If change were needed, as many of these women acknowledged it might be, it must come from inside the community of believers and operate within the terms of their discourse; it could not be imposed from outside, by the state. In an article in *Le Monde*'s magazine on September 9, 2005, a Muslim woman who began wearing the veil when she was seventeen and who considered herself a militant feminist called for an "evolution of mentalities." "They try to lead us to a normative vision of women's emancipation. But it's necessary to understand that there's not just one form of emancipation. If one champions a woman's liberty, then she ought to be given the liberty to make her own choices and not be imagined as some kind of idiot manipulated by her father or brother or the Saudi state. The French are thirty years behind in their perception of the veil."[40] Here the veil is taken to be thoroughly modern, although it does not conform to prevailing French notions of modernity.

Bouzar and Kada end their book with a plea, not for tolerance, but for recognition of the fact that current forms of Islam also provide a route to modernity for many young French women and men. And, they continue, the kind of person one is, the values one learns as a Muslim, are not antithetical or dangerous to the coherence and future of France. Indeed, the stress on ethical conduct, family relationships, education, social obligations, and reason produces subjects inclined to cooperation, not separation. It has been bipolar divisions like modern/traditional, secular/religious, West/East, French/Muslim, native/foreigner that have led to the isolation and marginalization of Muslim communities. Such divisions serve to justify the requirement of assimilation and, in so doing, rule out other ways to conceive of integration. But the French model of assimilation, Bouzar and Kada argue, is not the only way to think about integration. One doesn't necessarily have "a choice to make" between one's national identity and one's spiritual commitments. Citing French sociologist Emile Durkheim's now classic notion of organic solidarity, Bouzar and Kada talk of the interdependence and complementarity of a people whose commonality rests precisely on their need for one another, despite (or because of) their irreducible differences. In this I hear an echo of Jean-Luc Nancy's idea that difference is exactly what constitutes our "being-in-common." From Bouzar and Kada's perspective, integration without assimilation (as I suggested at the end of chapter 3) is within the scope of very French conceptions of society.

Bouzar and Kada remind readers, too, that Muslims have long had a place in France; they are already part of the nation, although their history remains to be written: "We are five million French Muslims waiting at the portals of the history of France."[41]

It is not for nothing that these young people battle for recognition of a shared history: an official acknowledgment of the colonial period, of the war in Algeria and of the sacrifice their grandparents made during the Second World War. It's not only a question of justice, of France avowing its debt, but also a profoundly symbolic question of common memory. These young people who are asked every day to prove their Frenchness want to remind us that their ancestors *are already* a part of French history.[42]

Already formally citizens, already acceptable as soldiers in wartime, already included as workers and taxpayers. Already an integral part of French history, despite religious beliefs that seem to be at odds with abstract individualism but that are, in essence, no different from the nonindividualist stances of other religions long considered compatible with French republicanism. Asked the woman interviewed by *Le Monde*, "When will it be understood that France is culturally diverse? That the veil is not a phenomenon foreign to France, but a French phenomenon?" These headscarf wearers insist that there is no incompatibility between being French and being the kind of person for whom spiritual values are essential. These are values, they maintain, that no more nor less than the values of secular individualism are compatible with the kind of learning and reasoning offered in French public schools.

Conclusion

By insisting, against evidence to the contrary, that girls in headscarves were either victims of their families or dupes of radical political Islamists, those supporting the headscarf ban represented themselves as agents of emancipation. They were at once saving the girls from the claims of an outmoded "culture" and protecting the republic from challenges to its sovereignty. While the girls and many of the opponents of the law maintained that the headscarf might represent an expression of individual conviction—one that was protected by the French constitution—the lawmakers insisted that this could not logically be the case. By definition, the headscarf was an endorsement of submission, an abandonment of individuality, and a declaration of one's primary allegiance to communal standards and obligations. It was a flag of a different color and, as such, signaled disloyalty to the principles and values of the republic. Realizing that this was the charge being made against them, and eager to refute it, a number of girls donned headscarves in the red, white, and blue stripes of the French flag. This way of symbolizing their existence as French Muslims—the compatibility of the two identities—was a gesture of conciliation that the lawmakers refused. Instead they held steadfastly to the caricatures they had created, both of Islam and of the republic: one a homogeneous culture or community, the other a homogeneous nation of individuals; one whose difference made its inclusion impossible, the other which recognized no difference at all.

By outlawing the headscarf, the state declared those who espoused Islam, in whatever form, to be literally foreigners to the French way of life. The law did not extend to adult women or to female university students (as adults they were granted the right to express their religious beliefs), but it did stigmatize them. Even though it did not apply at all to men or boys, they too were meant to understand that adherence to Islam was an obstacle to full integration. The refusal of Islam was all-encompassing; no distinctions were made about the kinds of beliefs held or the practices engaged in. In the categorical representation of Islam as an unchanging, tradition-bound religious culture, it was not possible to see the strains of modernity that Roy and others have pointed out, nor was it possible to see the similarities between Islamic and other religiosities. In this way the law objectified Muslims, designating a community where one had not existed before. "The more Islam is attacked," one educator declared, "the more women will wear the veil to defend Islam."[43] "France, by claiming to fight against communalism, actually increases it," added another commentator. "I don't know if the leaders realize the consequences their decision risks."[44]

Another facet of this process was the objectification of the republic as the embodiment of immutable principles; to question its particular forms or practices was to imperil the very existence of the nation. The effect was not only to silence all critics of the law (and of discrimination against Muslims, Arabs, North Africans) by declaring them enemies of the republic but also to render nonnegotiable exactly that which had to be negotiated: the integration of different individuals and different kinds of individuality into a nation which had never been as homogeneous as its self-styled representatives claimed it to be.

5

SEXUALITY

The law banning headscarves in public schools made a clear distinction between acceptable and unacceptable signs of religious conviction.

> The clothing and religious signs prohibited are *conspicuous* [*ostensible*] signs, such as a large cross, a veil, or a skullcap. Not regarded as signs indicating religious affiliation are *discreet* [*discret*] signs, which can be, for example, medallions, small crosses, stars of David, hands of Fatima, or small Korans.

I have drawn attention to the words "conspicuous" and "discreet" because they resolved the difficulty the Stasi commission and its advisors had in articulating what they were after. As is usual in political debate of this kind, there was a great deal of disagreement among legislators and others about the exact wording to use in the law. For a long time, the talk was of banning "ostentatious" signs, but that word was dropped because it ascribed motives to the wearer of the sign that might be difficult to prove. Then there was the word "visible"; the head of the National Assembly committee recommended that all "visible signs" of religious affiliation be banned from public schools. His colleagues demurred, largely because they thought the prohibition of all visible emblems was too broad and would conflict with the European Court's rulings that protected religious expression as an individual right. "Conspicuous" seemed a good alternative because it attributed the meaning of the sign to the sign itself; there was something objective about it and yet objectionable. It was more than visible; it was, well, conspicuous. The legislators opted for "discreet" as a way of distinguishing acceptable from unacceptable signs, since visibility could still be an ambiguous notion (things that are conspicuous, after all, are also visible).

One of many commentators pointed to the futility of these academic distinctions: it might be possible abstractly to separate "ostentatious," "conspicuous," and "visible," he said, but in practice it would be very difficult to distinguish among them.[1] Still, I think the effort is worth our attention, not so much because it exemplifies the obsessive concern with language that one thinks of as characteristically French, but because it reveals the hidden preoccupations that directed the discussion. I was struck in particular by the sexual connotations carried by the words the lawmakers chose. When "ostentatious" or "conspicuous" refers to an excessive display on or by a body, especially if it's a woman's body, it conveys a sense of erotic provocation. "Discreet" is the opposite of ostentatious or conspicuous: a discreet object doesn't call attention to itself; it downplays the attractiveness of the body in question; it is somehow neutral—asexual. In the opposition between "conspicuous" and "discreet," the language of the law intensified its philosophical disapproval of the headscarves' violation of laïcité with a veiled reference to unacceptable sexuality. There was something sexually amiss about girls in headscarves; it was as if both too little and too much were being revealed.

But in what way "too much"? After all, according to the girls who wore them, headscarves signified modesty and sexual unavailability. In the Muslim juristic tradition, "ostentation" was to be avoided at all costs. The Moroccan-Arabic word invoked by theologians is *tabarruj*. Abdellah Hammoudi tells us that it means "ostentatious," and it is "the invariable term for a bearing that is deemed immodest or conspicuous."[2] There is another Arabic word, *fitna*, adds anthropologist Saba Mahmood, that means both sexual temptation and the disruption of political order. Women were assumed to be objects of male sexual desire and thus inherently provocative, "an assumption that has come to justify the injunction that women should 'hide their charms' when in public so as not to excite the libidinal energies of men who are not their immediate kin." The goal of modest dress for women was to prevent such excitement.[3] By what standard could girls wearing headscarves be considered immodest or conspicuous? They did stand out in a classroom filled with girls in Western dress, but not because their clothing was more revealing. If anything, it was more discreet; more of the body was covered. How then account for this seemingly strange reversal? Muslim modesty is taken to be sexually aberrant by French observers, who condemn it not only as different but as somehow excessive (ostentatious, conspicuous), even perverse. The reason given by politicians and many feminists was the same: the veil represented the subordination of women, their humiliation, and their inequality. It must not be sanctioned by those who believed in the republican principles of liberty and equality. I don't think that this is a sufficient explanation for the kind of disturbing sexual connotation the veil had for its critics. It was not the absence of sexuality but its presence that was being remarked—a presence underlined by the girls' refusal to engage in what were taken to be the "normal" protocols of interaction with members of the opposite sex.

The veil's disturbing sexual connotation for French observers stemmed from its significance in a system of gender relations they took to be entirely different from their own. For Muslims, the veil is a declaration of the need to curb the dangerous sexuality of women (and also of men), a response, as Hammoudi puts it, "to the risks associated with [our] vital impulses." It is a recognition of the threat sex poses for society and politics. In contrast, the French system celebrates sex and sexuality as free of social and political risk. At the same time, sex poses a tremendous difficulty for the abstract individualism that is the basis for French republicanism: if we are all the same, why has sexual difference been such an obstacle to real equality? I will argue in this chapter that the headscarf pointed up this contradiction in the French gender system: Islam's insistence on recognizing the difficulties posed by sexuality revealed more than republicans wanted to see about the limits of their own system.

It is important to note here that it is idealized gender systems I am talking about. These, of course, have some relationship to how people behave and perceive one another, but they are not as fixed or all-encompassing as they seem. Like any categorization, they overstate prescriptive norms and underestimate the diversity of practices individuals actually engage in. It is the work of representation these idealized concepts do that I am interested in; because even for those who do not follow them to the letter, they offer a powerful point of reference around which understandings of difference are organized. Here again we see the objectification of Islam, on the one side, and France, on the other: Islam is seen as a system that oppresses women, French republicanism as one that liberates them.

The French who supported the headscarf ban talked in terms of a conflict between emancipatory modernity and oppressive tradition. Even though the French schoolgirls who chose to wear headscarves did so not as members of traditional societies or communities, they did accept a distinction they attributed to Islam. I would say that they wanted to operate in a discursive system different from the French one in which they found themselves. In the terminology offered by sociologist Farhad Khosrokhavar, the difference is between an "open" approach to gender relations and a "covered" one, both terms referring to the treatment of the sexed body. In "covered" systems, gender relations are regulated by codes of modesty. "Modesty and honor are defined in direct relation to the bodily and mental covering-over of the woman (the woman as the shield of honor for the community; the woman as manager of private space, closed to public space)." If traditionally, the order of the family and the purity of the entire social body rested on the separation of the sexes, for young Muslim girls in France it was their own bodily integrity, their own honor, that was at stake. In contrast, "open" systems are those which don't see the exposure of the body, its visibility, as detrimental. In these systems, "a certain type of voyeurism and exhibitionism . . . is positively valued. . . . The language of the body is that of its accessibility to the other sex."[4]

As Western feminists have often pointed out, uncovered

bodies are no more a guarantee of equality than covered ones. In both societies or systems women have been deemed inferior to men and their legal rights have been restricted, though it is certainly true that many societies with "open" systems have by now granted some measure of formal equality to women. In France, despite the bitter opposition of the same politicians who passed the headscarf ban in the name of women's rights, there is even a law on the books (enacted in 2000) that calls for equal numbers of women and men on the ballots in almost all elections. But the parity law, as it is called, has not stopped the devaluing of women that reduces them to their sex, and that led the Socialist Party colleagues of politician Ségolène Royal to try to check her presidential ambitions by reminding her that the race for the presidency "is not a beauty contest."

Until their ideological confrontation with Islam, many French feminists saw the sexual exhibitionism of their society—particularly as it applied to women—as demeaning to women because it reduced them to a sexed body. But in the heat of the headscarf controversy, those concerns were set aside and equality became synonymous with sexual emancipation, which in turn was equated with the visibility of the female body. As was the case with laïcité and autonomous individualism, the French system of gender was offered as not only the best, but the only acceptable, way to organize relations between the sexes. Those who did not conform to it were by definition inferior and therefore could never be fully French. The issue of covered or uncovered sexuality, I want to argue, gave the headscarf affair both its resonance and its intensity. Here was proof of the irreconcilable difference between the "culture" of Islam and France.

Visibility

In the headscarf controversy, opponents of the veil were consumed with the idea that it denied what they referred to as
mixité, the mixing of the sexes, in schools, hospitals, and elsewhere.[5] The veil, according to the Stasi commission (and to in-
numerable witnesses who appeared before it), was an expression of Islam's strict segregation of the sexes. In fact, at least in
the case of schools, the opposite was true: wearing a headscarf
allowed girls to attend coeducational schools who otherwise
would have been unable to. But the real concern of some of the
experts who testified to the Stasi commission was less mixité
than it was the same *visual* status for the bodies of women and
men. Hence, when psychoanalyst Elisabeth Roudinesco was
asked if she thought beards should be prohibited in schools,
since they could also be a form of Islamist identification, she
replied that there could be no legislation about beards. Not
only was such legislation impractical, but beards, even if worn
for religious reasons, did not constitute the same alienation for
men that veils did for women. Of course, beards have a lot to
do with sexuality; the difference was that beards were visible,
while women's bodies were disguised by veils. "I'm absolutely
convinced that the real problem posed by the veil is that it covers over [*il recouvre*] a sexual dimension. It denies the equality
between men and women upon which our society rests."[6] It
was precisely the covering over of women's sexuality that so
troubled her: the veil was a denial, she said, of women as "objects of desire."[7] Roudinesco was not bothered only by the veil's
association with women's inequality, a contradiction of a specific republican principle. She also thought the veil interfered

with what she took to be a natural psychological process: the
visual appreciation of women's bodies by men brought women's
femininity into being.

In this view, girls were lost to their feminine identity if their
bodies could not be seen. Identity was conferred by men's
being able to see them as sexual objects. Feminine identity
depended on male desire; male desire depended on visual stim-
ulation. Stasi talked of the veil as "objectively" alienating
women, not only from the exercise of their fundamental rights,
but also from their own sexuality, and Iranian feminist Chahdortt Djavann, one of many refugees from an Islamist theocracy, called the veil a form of "psychological, sexual and social
mutilation." It denied a young girl any possibility of "becoming
a human being."[8] Mutilation was a big preoccupation for many
commentators. Some even equated wearing the veil with geni-
tal mutilation.[9] Philosopher André Glucksmann described the
veil as "stained with blood" (a reference to terrorists and Nazis,
but also with inevitable connotations of cutting).[10] The logic of
Glucksmann's observation seemed to go like this: terrorism
constitutes the breaking of all the rules of political deportment;
veiling violates the rules of gendered interaction; the rules of
gendered interaction are the basis of social and political order;
therefore, veiling is terrorism.

According to this logic, it was difficult to maintain the view
that Muslim girls and women were victims; wearing the headscarf itself became an act of aggression. Jacques Chirac said as
much in a speech in Tunisia in December 2003. "Wearing the
veil, whether it is intended or not, is a kind of aggression."[11] In
this comment, Chirac was conflating terrorism and the veil
with an oblique reference to the hidden danger of women's re-

pressed sexuality. Out there to see, women's sexuality was manageable; unseen, it might wreak havoc—political as well as social.

But Chirac was also saying something else. The aggression he referred to was twofold: that of the veiled woman but also of the (Western) man trying to look at her. The aggression of the woman consisted in denying (French) men the pleasure—understood as a natural right (a male prerogative)—to see behind the veil. This was taken to be an assault on male sexuality, a kind of castration. Depriving men of an object of desire undermined the sense of their own masculinity. Sexual identity (in the Western or "open" model) works both ways: men confirm their sexuality not only by being able to look at—to openly desire—women but also by receiving a "look" from women in return. The exchange of desirous looks, the availability of faces for reading, is a crucial aspect of gender dynamics in "open" systems.

Headscarves don't actually cover the faces of their wearers; they cover their hair and ears and necks, but the faces are plainly visible. Despite this fact, commentators conflated women in the Gulf States with those in France and insisted on referring to headscarves as if they covered *faces*. For example, when the French media figure Bernard Henri Lévy was interviewed on National Public Radio in the United States about (among other things) the headscarf ban, his clinching point concerned the face. After listing a number of objections to the "veil" and explaining the need for a law banning it in public schools, he ended by talking about how sad it was to cover the beautiful faces of young girls—that in the end was Islam's worst offense. His remark is at first perplexing, for the faces of the girls in question were not actually covered. It becomes clear, though, when we realize that the uncovered face stands for the visibility of the entire body and, more importantly, its sexual availability. In this reasoning a body whose contours cannot be seen becomes a hidden face. So it's understandable that Lévy confuses the headscarf and the veil, not because both are variations on a Muslim style of dress, but because both signify modesty and the sexual unavailability of the woman. That unavailability is profoundly disturbing to the way identity is lived by French women and men.

While Lévy seemed bemused and saddened by being deprived of the sight of female beauty, another common response is aggression. Here is the way the psychiatrist Frantz Fanon, writing in the 1950s, described male colonizers' attitudes to veiled women in Algeria:

> there is also in the European the crystallization of an aggressiveness, the strain of a kind of violence before the Algerian woman. Unveiling this woman is revealing her beauty; it is baring her secret, breaking her resistance, making her available for adventure. . . . In a confused way, the European experiences his relation with the Algerian woman at a highly complex level. There is in it the will to bring this woman within his reach, to make her a possible object of possession. This woman who sees without being seen frustrates the colonizer. There is no reciprocity. She does not yield herself, does not give herself, does not offer herself.[12]

In the 1950s this "will to bring women within reach" had to do with the sexualized fantasies of colonial domination that I discussed in chapter 2: white men conquering indigenous women. In the new century, it has to do with a perceived attack on (aggression against) what its French defenders insist is the right way (perhaps the only way) to conduct relations between the sexes. It is no longer the conquest of a new territory that is at stake, but the (aggressive) defense of the homeland, of the republican principles of liberty and equality. A distinctively French form of sexuality was even posited as a trait of national character. It was, in historian Mona Ozouf's words, "la singularité française (the French singularity)."[13]

In what can only be described as a burst of nationalist fervor, many French feminists took up the cry for the liberation of Muslim women, forgetting their own critique of the visual exploitation they had protested in the past. To be sure, during the "string" affair (see chapter 3), objections were voiced to the oversexualized style young girls had adopted. Ségolène Royal, for example, warned that "in the eyes of boys, the string reduces young girls to a behind."[14] She and others cautioned that the tyranny of this fashion was not liberating, but they did not go as far as some American critics—students of Islam—who questioned the superiority of "open" to "covered" ways of dressing: "Can our bras, ties, pants, miniskirts, underwear and bathing suits all be so easily arrayed on one side or another of [the] divide" between freedom and captivity?[15] Aren't there, instead, two different systems of subjection at play?

Aside from one or two articles equating the veil and the string as two sides of the same oppressive coin, there was not much discussion in France of the limits of Western dress. It was the veil that must be removed in the name of equality. Not,

I would argue, the equality of women and men, but that of Muslim *women* and French *women*. Although, of course, there were many types of Muslim women, some veiled and some not, and many types of French women as well, the representation of this issue offered only two contrasting categories. The point was to bring Muslim women up to the standard of their French sisters (a version of the civilizing mission with all of its racist and colonial implications), free to display their bodies and experience the joys of sex—as French society (women and men) understood them. Minister of the interior Nicolas Sarkozy said precisely this in 2005: "We are proud of the values of the Republic, of equality between men and women, of laïcité, and of the French ideal of integration. So let us dare to speak of these to those we welcome here. And let us bring pressure to bear so that the rights of French women apply also to immigrant women."[16]

Sexual Freedom

On the eve of the passage of the headscarf ban, the feminist political scientist Janine Mossuz-Lavau wrote an eloquent appeal against the law. "When I pass a woman with a veil in the street," her article began, "I feel a pang of emotion." Not, she explained, because she was hostile to the woman's religion, but because the veil designated the woman as "a source of sin," and "as a potential whore." As such she was "prohibited from sex with anyone but her husband or future husband." Mossuz-Lavau felt deeply for this woman, deprived as she was of the sexual liberation that was hers by right.

But such liberation, the sociologist went on, could only

come from being exposed to modern ideas at school. Indeed, public opinion polls demonstrated that modern liberal attitudes were held by those with high levels of education; the most bigoted members of French society were those with no degrees. Mossuz Lavau then cited a study she had done in 2000–2001 of sexual practices in French society. Of the Muslim women she interviewed, "the only ones who transgressed [Islamic] norms and who had sexual relations before marriage were students and managers with advanced degrees." "These young women refused the dictate of virginity until marriage and it was no accident that all of them had . . . a higher education." If the test of liberation were sexual freedom, she concluded, then girls with headscarves must be allowed to stay in school. "I think that school, at whatever level, can have this function and will aid those who are permitted to remain there to direct themselves to a freer life."[17]

Chahdortt Djavann, whose claim to expertise was her own experience in Iran, offered sensationalist tales of women's lack of freedom in Muslim countries. That neither she nor her most attentive followers distinguished among different Islams—Islam as a state religion in a theocracy run by mullahs is not the same as the minority religion followed by those living in France—is indicative of the hysteria that informed much of the debate. Djavann stated not only that women were oppressed in "Islamic societies" but also (in terms reminiscent of some of the colonial attitudes I described in chapter 2) that the separation of the sexes necessarily gave rise to rape and prostitution. It was as if the veil, by designating women as dangerously licentious, encouraged the attacks. Pedophilia, too, was common: "if relations sexual, nonsexual, and nonconjugal between two con-

senting adults are prohibited and severely sanctioned by Islamic laws, no law protects the children."[18] In her accounts,
neither women nor children were spared the attention of
predatory males, an attention stimulated by the sharp segregation of the sexes. All of Islam was organized on these men's behalf, she maintained. Only a law banning headscarves would
prevent similar developments in France. This law, she believed,
might even offer hope to women in theocratic regimes such as
Iran. Absent from Djavann's discussion was any acknowledgment of the complexity of life in Iran (where, as I have already
mentioned, women vote and serve in parliament even if they
wear veils) or of the existence of mistreatment of women in
France. As feminist sociologist Christine Delphy put it, Muslims do not have a monopoly on the abuse of women.[19]

Although Mossuz-Lavau and Djavann differed on the question of the wisdom of the law, they shared a belief in the innate
desire of women for emancipation in Western terms. It was
clear to them that women would not choose the veil unless
they were forced to. This was the position also taken by Ni
Putes, Ni Soumises (Neither Whores nor Subjected), a group
of feminists that included many who had lived under Islamist
regimes. The group was formed in 2002 to protest physical violence against women perpetrated in the name of Islam. In a
widely circulated petition they supported the ban on headscarves because "the Islamic veil subjects all of us, Muslim and
non-Muslim alike, to an intolerable discrimination against
women."[20] This outlook stunned the two Muslim women who
coauthored *One Veiled, the Other Not*. Dounia Bouzar, who did
not wear a veil, nonetheless marveled at the misunderstanding
of Islam contained in the standard of liberation offered by

A cartoon that appeared at the time of the "string" affair. The words read: I wouldn't want to be in her place. Cartoon by Catherine Beaunez, used with her permission.

French feminists. "The leitmotif of their messages revolves around the idea that when Muslim women are free to sleep with as many men as they want to, then they will be integrated. Liberty is measured by the number of sexual acts they engage in." Saïda Kada reminded Bouzar of the first images to appear in France of the liberation of Kabul. "Women putting on make-up. What symbolism: from the burqa to lipstick! They [the French] were reassured not about the well-being of hu manity but about the capacity of women to live up to Western models."[21]

Bouzar's point about integration is telling. She rightly perceives that sexual liberation is at the heart of objections to the veil and to Islam more generally. It is not simply a question of individual autonomy being hampered by communal loyalty or religious prescription interfering with the secular construction of the self. The self the legislators and their feminist supporters imagined was not only sexed but sexual; not only sexual but sexually active in familiar ways. Commenting on a particularly scandalous set of events in the Muslim community in 1989 (two brothers had killed themselves after killing their sister, who had dated a French man; honor killings of this kind, though rare, were mistakenly attributed to Islam as such), the television journalist Christine Ockrent drew a moral conclusion: "This sordid story makes clear in an exaggerated fashion the difficulties, the tensions, the obscure innermost recesses of belonging to another culture where sexuality in particular is lived differently."[22] Jean Daniel, the editor of *Le Nouvel Observateur*, writing in 1986 about whether Islam could be transformed by its contact with "French civilization," noted that "the problem of women, of the woman, the problem of sexuality, counts enormously in this story."[23] Sexuality was the measure of difference, of the distance Muslims had to traverse if they were to become fully French.

The Clash of Gender Systems

When Elisabeth Roudinesco testified before the Stasi commission, she assured its members that a law banning headscarves was justified. In order to stress its urgency, she talked about it not as a routine piece of legislation but as a fundamental prohibition, equivalent to the laws against incest.[24] The reference to the incest taboo is revealing. It suggests a deep uneasiness evoked by Islam's different ways of regulating sex and sexuality. It expresses as well the idea that Islam was not regulating sexuality as it should, that something excessive, even perverse, was going on in Muslim communities and households. Incest, after all, is taken to be a deformation of what is universally moral, healthy, and natural. At the beginning of this chapter, I noted that many objections to the headscarf conveyed the feeling that not just too little but also too much was being revealed by it. Now it is time to return to that point.

French supporters of the ban on headscarves insisted that their notion of gender equality was not only French but (like the incest taboo) universally desirable. This was precisely the objection of some of the Muslim women I have cited; they refused the claim that the French system was necessarily more egalitarian, and they resented the caricature of their own beliefs. At issue was not just a conflict between "open" and "covered" cultures but a specifically French theory that addresses the relationship between abstract individualism and sexual difference. As I will explain in what follows, the French theory involves *denial* of the problem of reconciling those two concepts. In contrast, sexual difference is *recognized* as a potential political problem by Muslim theorists; the separation of the sexes is a way of addressing it. Ironically, Islamic theory puts sex out there as a problem for all to see by conspicuously covering the body, while the French call for a conspicuous display of bodies in order to deny the problem that sex poses for republican political theory. I will characterize the difference between Islam and French republicanism by referring to a psychology of recognition and a psychology of denial.

❖

By banning the headscarf, French legislators insisted they were removing *the* sign of women's inequality from the classroom and, in so doing, declaring that the equality of women and men was a first principle of the republic. Anyone who would pledge allegiance to the republic must endorse that principle. It was one of the tenets of laïcité. "Today, laïcité cannot be conceived without a direct link to equality between the sexes."[25] The discussions before the Stasi commission and elsewhere (in the press, on television, in various public forums) emphasized sexual self-expression as the primary test of equality, an expression consisting of what Mona Ozouf referred to as "happy exchanges between the sexes."[26] The visibility of the bodies of women and men, their easy accessibility to one another, the free play of seduction, were taken to be hallmarks of liberty and equality, the expression on the personal level of what it means to live in a politically free society. Sex was not dangerous to political intercourse (as Rousseau and other political theorists had once warned) but, on the contrary, a positive influence on it.

And yet women have long presented a challenge to French republican theorists, one that has become more difficult since they were granted the vote in 1945. Citizenship in France is based on abstract individualism. The individual is the essential human, regardless of religion, ethnicity, social position, or occupation. When they are abstracted from these traits, individuals are considered to be the same, that is, equal. Equality in the French system rests on sameness. The one obstacle to sameness for many years was sexual difference: women were "the sex" and so could not be abstracted from their sex; men could be so abstracted. Hence, abstract individuals were synonymous with men. The sexual difference of women was taken to be a natural distinction and therefore not susceptible to abstraction. How then could women be citizens? The history of French feminism demonstrates how difficult it was to grapple with this dilemma: women must strive for abstraction in order to become equal (the same as men), but the difference of their sex (they were not men) disqualified them in advance. Can women be the same and yet different? Well, yes and no. Yes, because according to republican political theory, citizens are abstract individuals, indistinguishable from one another. So once women are citizens, they are individuals. No, because by definition, sexual difference means that not all individuals are the same; nature has decreed a lack of sameness (an inequality) that society cannot correct. Men can escape their sex; women cannot. There is then a deep incompatibility between the reasoning of political theory and the dilemma posed by sexual difference; sexual difference does not seem susceptible to republican logic.

When women got the vote, it was as a particular group, not as individuals. In the recent debates about the parity law, the heterosexual couple was offered as a substitute for the singular individual. Men and women could complement each other in their difference, it was suggested, and this complementarity was a kind of equality. But just as the division of labor between husbands and wives in marriages has hardly produced regimes of perfect equality, so that division imported into politics keeps creating difficulties for women who want to run for office. The brutal treatment of Ségolène Royal (which persisted even after her nomination by the Socialists) is not the worst example of its kind. Both notions—citizens who were women, not individuals, and the complementarity of difference—were put forward to correct, but not to alter, the bottom line of French republicanism: equality is still based on sameness. (This idea that sameness is a prerequisite for equality, of course, is what leads to the insistence on assimilation as a passport to Frenchness.)

There is, then, a persistent contradiction in French political theory between political equality and sexual difference. Politicians and republican theorists have dealt with this contradiction by covering it over, by insisting that equality is possible while elevating the differences between the sexes to a distinctive cultural character trait—Ozouf's "singularité française." As if to prove that women cannot be abstracted from their sex (men, of course, can be), there is great emphasis on the visibility and openness of seductive play between women and men, and especially on the public display (and sexual desirability for men) of women's bodies. The demonstrable proof of women's difference has to be out there for all to see, at once a confirmation of the need for different treatment of them *and* a denial of the problem that sex poses for republican political theory. We might say then that, paradoxically, the objectification of women's sexuality serves to veil a constitutive contradiction of French republicanism. This is what I mean by the psychology of denial.

Islamic jurists deal with sexual difference in a way that

avoids the contradiction of French republicanism by acknowledging directly that sex and sexuality pose problems (for society, for politics) that must be addressed and managed. The systems of address and management vary (neither the Taliban nor the ayatollahs of Iran represent all of Islam), and they may not seem acceptable to Western observers, but we do not have to accept them to understand what the dynamic is and why it might be so upsetting to French republicans. Modest dress, represented by the headscarf or veil for women and loose clothing for men, is a way of recognizing the potentially volatile and disruptive effects of sexual relations between women and men, driven by impulses, Hammoudi says, "that are a source of continuity, but also of merciless dangers and conflicts."[27] Modest dress declares that sexual relations are off-limits in public places. Some Muslim feminists say this actually liberates them, but whether it does or not, or whether, indeed, every woman who wears a headscarf understands its symbolism in this way, the veil signals the acceptance of sexuality and even its celebration, but only under proper circumstances—that is, in private, within the family. This is a psychology not of denial but of recognition.

I do not mean to say that the system is not patriarchal; it is, of course. But the French system is patriarchal too; women are objectified in both systems, although in different ways. My point is that sex and sexuality are differently represented, differently managed in these two systems. Paradoxically, for Islam it is the veil that makes explicit—available for all to see—the rules of public gendered interaction, which are in no way contradictory and which declare sexual exchanges out of bounds in public space. It is this explicit acknowledgment of the problem of sexuality that, for French observers, makes the veil ostentatious or conspicuous in the sexual sense of those words. Not only is too much being said about sex, but all of its difficulties are being revealed. Women may be formally equal, but the difference of their sex somehow belies that equality. The pious pronouncements of French politicians about the equality of men and women are at odds with their deep uneasiness about actually sharing power with the opposite sex. These are difficulties that theorists and apologists for French republicanism want to deny.

The power of the psychology of denial is what led so many French feminists to abandon their critique of the status quo in France and rush to support a law that offered laïcité as the ground for gender equality. It would take another book to analyze the reasons for the abandonment of the themes of job and wage discrimination, glass ceilings, and domestic violence—what some have referred to as the "exhaustion" of the militant feminism of the 1970s and 80s. Suffice it to say here that—in a kind of racist benevolence reminiscent of some of their predecessors—feminists turned to the salvation of their less fortunate immigrant sisters. (Their insistence on bringing emancipation to these benighted women reminds us of Laura Bush's defense of the war on Afghanistan as an effort to liberate the women there.) Entirely forgotten in the glorification of the freedom of French sexual relations was the critique of these same feminists, who for years have decried the limits of their own patriarchal system, with its objectification of women and overemphasis on their sexual attractiveness. It is the power of their unconscious identification with the republican project—their own acceptance of the psychology of denial—that led many of them to unequivocally condemn the headscarf/veil as a violation of women's rights and to talk as if the status of women in France were not a problem at all. Banning the headscarf became an act of patriotism. "By rising up against 'foreign' signs of sexism," wrote Christine Delphy sarcastically, "doesn't our society prove that it won't tolerate sexism? Therefore, that it isn't sexist? . . . The difference of others as sexists is confirmed while the absence of sexism among us is proof of the foreignness of the sexists."[28] The conclusive evidence of the inassimilability of Muslims was the difference of their approach to sex and sexuality.

Conclusion

The preservation of a mythical notion of "France" in its many aspects was a driving force in the *affaires des foulards*. The deep psychic investments revealed by the issue were less about fears of terrorism (there were surely better ways to deal with terrorism than banning the headscarf, some of which were suggested by the various commissions) than about defending French national identity—an identity in which the French way of addressing the relations between the sexes was a critical, inviolable component. Indeed, as sociologist Eric Fassin has noted, the new emphasis (only about ten years old) on the foundational nature of sexual equality is a way of insisting on the immutability of the republic in its current incarnation. Sexual equality (like laïcité) has become a primordial value. Those who don't share this value (Muslims in this case) are not only different but inferior—less evolved, if capable at all of evolution. The ultimate proof of the inassimilablity of Islam thus comes down, or adds up, to sexual incompatibility. This incompatibility was so profound that it compromised the future of the nation—its literal reproductive future as well as its representation. "One and indivisible" might include men and women, but it couldn't accommodate more than one arrangement of the relations between them because the existing arrangement was said to be rooted not just in culture but in nature. The French gender system was represented, then, as not only superior but "natural." Hence the profound psychological repugnance for a way of being whose difference, from this perspective, could only be perverse.

CONCLUSION

Each year the French National Assembly gives an award to the best book about politics published in the preceding year. In 2006, its choice was *La tentation obscurantiste* (*The Obscurantist Temptation*) by Caroline Fourest.[1] Fourest is a feminist, one of the founders of the journal *ProChoix* (*Pro-Choice*) and a leading supporter of the headscarf ban. She has been a fierce opponent of what she calls religious fundamentalisms and a staunch advocate of laïcité. To characterize her secularism as absolutist is an understatement: she sees it as the only weapon that can protect us from the loss of freedom and self-determination that religious activists will impose the minute they get the chance. When I met her in New York several years ago, she and her then-partner Fiammetta Venner were tracking the international networks of Christian evangelical groups based in the United States. I shared their concern about the impact these groups were having on women, especially access to abortion and contraception, and we worried together about the political power they had acquired here (it was just before George W. Bush was elected for the first time). For Fourest and Venner, religious extremism was the most virulent form patriarchy could take, and they felt feminists must make combating it a first priority.

Soon after I met them, their attention turned to Islam. They raised a cry of alarm about what seemed to them to be an increase in the influence of "fundamentalists" among French Muslims. As the law on headscarves was being debated in 2003, they devoted whole issues of their journal to rallying faithful secularists to their campaign on its behalf. Unlike the careful distinctions they had made between mainstream Christians or Jews and extremists of those faiths, they tended to treat Islam as monolithic, by definition entirely extremist. They insisted that Islamists were engaged in a political conspiracy the aim of which was the oppression of women and the elimination of secularism—in short, that the experience of Iran was about to be imported into France. "The veil is not a debate in itself. It is a test which ought to allow us to affirm a particularly ambitious vision of laïcité at a moment when it is more threatened than ever by the rise of fundamentalisms."[2] There might be some Muslims who didn't fit this description, but they were few. And they were not among those wearing headscarves.

Fourest and Venner were vehement about headscarves, which they always referred to as veils. They considered them enemy flags in a war to the death with fanaticism. "The authorization of the veil in schools is only one step in the agenda of fundamentalist associations which want to test secularism."[3] They furiously rejected the charge made by some of their former associates that they were "Islamaphobes." There was not a shred of racism, they insisted, in their defense of laïcité. Those who made such accusations were naive, or worse, dupes of a dangerous cultural relativism. Like the articles she and Venner wrote, Fourest's book lashes out against those who consider themselves serious students of Islam and who insist, as I have, on the complexity of the experience of Muslims in France. She dismisses them as fifth columnists, conspiring with the enemy to undermine the republic.

When the prize for Fourest's book was announced, a group of intellectuals wrote an op-ed piece to protest it in *Le Monde* (April 18, 2006). They included Jean Baubérot and Etienne Balibar. The authors called Fourest's arguments reductive and unfounded, designed to demonize an "other" rather than to shed light on the serious challenge posed by the need to better integrate "immigrants" into French society. They regretted that the prize officially endorsed a polemic that was fraudulent in its arguments and that played to fear and emotion instead of reason. The article is bitter, offering a brief but cogent critique of what has been long-standing government policy. Though they express dismay at the National Assembly's choice of this book, they are not really surprised by it, for the book simply repeats what the legislators have been saying for years. Fourest has become, like many of them, an ideologue waving a nationalist banner; in the name of Enlightenment principles, she closes the door on discussion and refuses to entertain opinions other than her own.

The Assembly's endorsement of Fourest's book shows how the campaign has worked: those supporting the republicanist position have received great official and media attention while its critics have been neglected or even censored. More than one group has protested its inability to gain access to mainstream media or to any kind of public forum. In one case, the Union of Secular Families (l'Union des familles laïques) successfully prevailed upon mayors to prevent the screening in their towns of a film called *A Barely Veiled Racism*, which sympathetically presents the views of those who opposed the headscarf ban. In the name of truth or history or nature, a vision of the republic has been put forward which makes sacred and incontestable the founding principles of abstract individualism, secularism, and an "open" gender system. These principles are offered as a test of the true faith of French citizens. Those who do not subscribe to them are treated as infidels.

By honoring *La Tentation obscurantiste* with an award, the government continued its campaign against headscarves. The law has been in effect since 2004, and, it seems, most Muslims have accommodated to the rules. For many poor families there was no choice since welfare payments are tied to children's school attendance. Those who haven't complied have been expelled; some have gone elsewhere, often to private schools, where the ban is not in force. The initial protests against the law (one girl in Strasbourg shaved her head: if she couldn't cover her hair, she'd get rid of it entirely) have ceased, or at least they are no longer drawing the attention of the media. But the law has not won Muslims to secularism; if anything, the numbers and kinds of veils evident in some neighborhoods have increased. Even if students remove their headscarves during school hours, they put them back on at the end of the day. They are, thus, constantly reminded that their religiosity does not fit with the requirements of the French state, and have an experience, repeated daily, of difference and discrimination.

Although the law applies only to students in the equivalent of our public elementary and high schools, it has been taken as a more general expression of official disapproval of the veil. Adult women in headscarves have sometimes been barred from naturalization ceremonies, even though they had met the requirements. "At the prefecture of Bobigny," reported one woman seeking naturalization, "a woman told me that the veil was not accepted by French society, that my case would be compromised if I kept it on." Mayors have sometimes denied social services to veiled women on the (mistaken) grounds that wearing the hijab is against the law. Women have been told that they cannot serve as witnesses at weddings, or, indeed, even get married. "At Montfermeil, and at Blanc-Mesnil, they refused to perform a marriage ceremony because of my veil. And yet my face was not covered." In many cases, court officials have not allowed women in headscarves to be sworn in or even to attend trials. Veiled women have, similarly, been turned away by employers. "The veil is a 100 percent handicap in French society. You don't see veiled women [working] anywhere, even at the checkout counters of supermarkets in our neighborhoods. In the end it's not because of Islam that we stay at home, but because of French society." One woman recounted her experience at a bank, where a teller refused to wait on her because her veil might be the disguise for a hold-up. Another, the mother of five children, who was elected a delegate of the parents' association at her son's school reported: "With the parents, I never had any problems. But the teachers refused to listen to me. They were obsessed by my headscarf. One of them finally told me that wearing it was forbidden."[4] On the basis of these testimonies, we might conclude that rather than resolving the problem of integrating Muslims into French society, the law banning headscarves has exacerbated it.

And indeed, the law has had ramifications well beyond the classrooms of French public schools. Passed as an endorsement of secularism and gender equality, it has in fact authorized expressions of racism and legitimized practices of discrimination. The riots in the fall of 2005 revealed the enormous discrepancy between the lives of "immigrants" and "French," the failure of schools to offer passports out of the banlieues, the persistent discrimination in the job market and consequently the huge differentials in unemployment rates between "immigrant" and "French" youth, the stigma attached to names, addresses, and other signs of North African (and increasingly, West African) origin. And the response of government officials—the denunciation of rioting, unemployed youth as "rabble," the attribution of blame for the uprisings to illegal residents and the move to expel them from France—signals once again a refusal to face the fact that this is a French problem. It is, moreover, a postcolonial French problem, not a foreign import.

In order to come to terms with its North African/Muslim population, French politicians and intellectuals need to come up with new ways of addressing difference, ways that acknowledge its existence rather than refusing to engage it. The old ways, the insistence on sameness and assimilation, aren't working. Instead of exploring what might be done, however, the nation's leaders have, for the most part, adhered to a myth of republican universalism that is as dogmatic as it is phantasmatic. The political hysteria that characterized the campaign to pass the headscarf law depicted the veil as a terrorist threat subverting the nation from within. In response the nation was rallied to a defense of the supposedly immutable principles of laïcité, abstract individualism, and (newly added, but taken also to be immutable) gender equality. If, as Emmanuel Terray has written, hysteria serves to deny and displace difficult realities, challenges to one's way of being that one doesn't want to face, then the law achieved its end. But only temporarily and with no good effect, for its primary impact was to reaffirm the unacceptable difference of Muslims in French society. Their place as outsiders or, more accurately, as insiders who don't belong was reaffirmed. The attribution of inferior otherness that George Fredrickson defines as racism was attached to the veil, and beyond it to everything Muslim, Arab, and North African. The headscarf law, then, was not so much a solution to a problem as a symptom of France's inability or unwillingness to face the racism—the continuing power imbalance based on ethnic/religious difference—that has characterized its dealings with North Africans for so long.

It is clear, as Charlotte Nordmann has written, that the myth of republican universalism operated as a veil "thrown over the relations of domination" between "native French" and French Muslims. Removing the Islamic headscarf was a way of insisting on assimilation as the only route to full membership in the community of the French. "If there is [a problem] of communalism, shouldn't we look for it on the side of the state? It's true that the majoritarian character of that communalism allows it to deny that fact and instead to pose as . . . the universal."[5] Put another way, we might say that absolutist secularism, undergirded by the idea that the French way of doing gender and sexuality was "natural," made it impossible to treat Muslim difference as a viable or normal way of being in the world.

The attack on the Islamic headscarf leaves another veil in place, one that covers over the contradiction between a highly particularistic ("singular") claim to a universalism that can and must only be French and the insistence on the elimination of difference (in this case, the difference of Islam) as the only viable way to maintain the integrity of the nation-state. What is the cost of this insistence on homogeneity? What is the definition of democracy it implies? These are the questions posed by the critics of the ban I have cited in these pages, among them Baubérot, Balibar, Gaspard, Khosrokhavar, and Nordmann. They argue that the notion of laïcité used to justify the law not only misrepresents France's own history of secularization but also exacerbates the social problems faced by current immigrant populations. The requirement of sameness underwrites and perpetuates racism.

In this way, the case of the French headscarf law is not just a local story. It allows us to think more broadly about the terms on which democratic polities (including our own) are organized and to analyze critically the ways in which the idea of a "clash of civilizations" undermines the very democracy it is meant to promote. Here the work of the American political philosopher Danielle Allen is pertinent, though her specific focus is on racial differences in the United States. Allen suggests that because the political idea of "oneness" (in France, the nation one and indivisible) requires unanimity, it produces exclusions that are contrary to democratic ideals of inclusiveness. She substitutes the concept of "wholeness" because it recognizes the existence of disagreement and differences within a "multitude of citizens" and thus opens the way for the kind of political engagement that negotiates rather than excludes. The key point in her work is that democracy requires a recognition of difference if some kind of commonality is to be achieved. "A full democratic politics should seek not only agreement, but also the democratic treatment of continued disagreement."[6] It is not, as the French lawmakers assumed, the sameness of all individuals that defines commonality, but the recognition of their difference. To return to a French source, the philosopher Jean-Luc Nancy, whom I cited in the introduction, the issue is not common being but being-in-common. Articulating this idea as the basis for democratic politics in the twenty-first century is undoubtedly a challenge for countries that have equated (cultural, religious, or ethnic) homogeneity with national identity. But as the populations of these countries become more diverse, "being-in-common" is the best alternative we have.

NOTES

Introduction

1. "Sondage exclusif: Intégration, voile et droits des femmes . . . Ce que veulent les musulmanes," *Elle*, December 15, 2003, pp. 78–94.

2. *New York Times*, November 18, 2006.

3. Cited at www.islamophobia-watch.com (entries under "women"). Bishop quote is from *ABC News*, August 28, 2005; De Cuyper, from *Indynews*, October 18, 2005.

4. Olivier Roy, *Globalized Islam: The Search for a New Ummah* (New York: Columbia University Press, 2004), p. 15.

5. Ibid., pp. 143, 151.

6. Nicolas Weill, "What's in a Scarf? The Debate on *Laïcité* in France," *French Politics, Culture and Society* 24, no. 1 (Spring 2006), pp. 59–73.

7. Although it does not seem to have figured explicitly in the debates, the word *fichu* also lurked in the collective unconscious. The term means a piece of cloth, but colloquially it refers to a scarf or babushka, some kind of head covering. *Fichu* is also used as an adjective to mean ruined or destroyed. Robert's dictionary gives an example: "with this bad weather, the picnic is ruined [*fichu*]." The association between headscarves and destruction could thus be evoked in a single word, making headscarves synonymous with disaster.

8. Wendy Brown, *Regulating Aversion: Tolerance in the Age of Identity and Empire* (Princeton: Princeton University Press, 2006).

9. Jean-Luc Nancy, "Of Being in Common," in Miami Theory

Collective, ed., *Community at Loose Ends* (Minneapolis: University of Minnesota Press, 1991), pp. 1–12; and Nancy, *The Inoperative Community* (Minneapolis: University of Minnesota Press, 1991).

1. The Headscarf Controversies

1. *Le Monde*, October 28, 1993.

2. *Le Monde*, October 17, 1989, and October 21, 1989; *Libération*, October 17, 1989.

3. *Le Nouvel Observateur*, November 2, 1989.

4. The full text of the council ruling, as of other official documents for 1989 and 1993–1994, can be found in *Laïcité française: Le port du voile à l'école républicaine*, 2 vols. (Paris: Fonds d'Action sociale pour les travailleurs immigrés et leurs familles, Service documentation, 1995). The pages are not sequentially numbered and the materials are not necessarily in chronological order, so I cannot direct the reader to a more precise location.

5. The text of the decree and responses to it are in *Laïcité française*. The comment on Chenière's crusade is in *Le Monde*, September 21, 1994.

6. "Neutralité de l'enseignement public," Circulaire Ministerielle no. 35, September 29, 1994.

7. *Le Monde* reported that Jewish leaders were assured by Prime Minister Balladur that "the yarmulke is not ostentatious." *Le Monde*, December 21, 1994.

8. See, for example, *Le Monde*, December 11, 1994, and the documents in *Laïcité française*.

9. Françoise Gaspard and Farhad Khosrokhavar, *Le foulard et la république* (Paris: La Découverte, 1995), p. 210.

10. Marc Howard Ross, "Dressed to Express: Islamic Headscarves in French Schools," paper presented to the Ethnohistory Program of the University of Pennsylvania, February 23, 2006.

11. The full texts were published as Bernard Stasi, *Laïcité et République: Rapport de la commission de réflexion sur l'application du principe de laïcité dans la République remis au Président de la République le 11 décembre 2003* (Paris: La Documentation française, 2004) and Jean-Louis Debré, *La laïcité à l'école: Un principe républicain à réaffirmer*. Rapport No. 1275, 2 vols. (Paris: Assemblée Nationale, 2003).

12. *Le Monde*, October 11, 2003.

13. Ibid.

14. *Le Monde*, September 25, 2003.

15. Alma and Lila Lévy, *Des filles comme les autres: Au-delà du foulard* (Paris: La Découverte, 2004), p. 62.

16. *Le Monde*, October 9, 2003.

17. *ProChoix*, no. 25 (Summer 2003), p. 22.

18. The quarrels can be followed in condensed (and intense) form in the pages of the feminist journal *ProChoix*, no. 25 (Summer 2003), nos. 26–27 (Autumn 2003), and no. 28 (Spring 2004).

2. Racism

1. George M. Fredrickson, *Racism: A Short History* (Princeton: Princeton University Press, 2002), p. 5.

2. Ibid., p. 9.

3. Cited in Edmund Burke III, "Theorizing the Histories of Colonialism and Nationalism in the Arab Maghrib," in Ali A. Ahmida, ed., *Beyond Colonialism and Nationalism in North Africa: History, Culture, and Politics* (London: St. Martin's Press, 2001), n. 9.

4. Cited in Olivier Le Cour Grandmaison, *Coloniser exterminer: Sur la guerre et l'état colonial* (Paris: Fayard, 2005), p. 99.

5. Edmond Burke III, "The Terror and Religion: Brittany and Algeria," in Gregory Blue, Martin Bunton, and Ralph Crozier, eds., *Colonialism and the Modern World Order* (New York: M. E. Sharpe, 2001).

6. Ibid., pp. 98–107.

7. Cited in Burke, "Theorizing," n. 6.

8. Neil MacMaster, *Colonial Migrants and Racism: Algerians in France, 1900–62* (New York: St. Martin's Press, 1996), p. 44.

9. Hafid Gafaiti, "Nationalism, Colonialism, and Ethnic Discourse in the Construction of French Identity," in Tyler Stovall and Georges Van Den Abeele, eds., *French Civilization and Its Discontents: Nationalism, Colonialism, Race* (Lanham, Md.: Lexington Books, 2003), p. 198.

10. Cited in Julia Clancy-Smith, "La Femme Arabe: Women and Sexuality in France's North African Empire," in Amira El Azhary Sonbol, ed., *Women, the Family, and Divorce Laws in Islamic History* (Syracuse, N.Y.: Syracuse University Press, 1996), p. 56.

11. Cited in MacMaster, *Colonial Migrants,* p. 44.

12. Henry Laurens, "La politique musulmane de la France," *Monde Arabe: Maghreb-Machrek*, no. 152 (April–June 1996), p. 8.

13. MacMaster, *Colonial Migrants,* p. 122.

14. Ibid., p. 91.

15. Ibid., p. 125.

16. Ibid., p. 127.

17. Ibid.

18. Ibid., p. 107.

19. Ibid., p.108.

20. Ibid., p. 114.

21. Ibid., p. 141.

22. Gabriel Esquer, *L'Algérie vue par les écrivains* (Oran: Simoun, 1959), p. 13.

23. Julia Clancy-Smith, "Islam, Gender, and Identities in the Making of French Algeria, 1830–1962," in Julia Clancy-Smith and Frances Gouda, eds., *Domesticating Empire: Race, Gender and Family Life in French and Dutch Colonialism* (Charlottesville: University of Virginia Press, 1998), p. 154.

24. Cited in Esquer, *L'Algérie*, p. 24.

25. Marnia Lazreg, *The Eloquence of Silence: Algerian Women in Question* (New York: Routledge, 1994), p. 49.

26. Malek Alloula, *The Colonial Harem*, trans. M. and W. Godzich (Minneapolis: University of Minnesota Press, 1986), p. 122. See also Christelle Taraud, *La prostitution coloniale: Algérie, Tunisie, Maroc (1830–1962)* (Paris: Payot, 2003), and Taraud, *Mauresques* (Paris: Albin Michel, 2003).

27. Lazreg, *The Eloquence of Silence*, pp. 31–33.

28. Ibid., p. 55.

29. Ibid., p. 57.

30. Hubertine Auclert, *Les femmes arabes en Algérie* (Paris: Société d'éditions littéraires, 1900), p. 6.

31. Alloula, *The Colonial Harem*, p. 21.

32. Auclert, *Les femmes arabes*, p. 24.

33. Clancy-Smith, "La Femme Arabe," p. 57.

34. Clancy-Smith, "Islam, Gender, and Identities," p. 159.

35. Auclert, *Les femmes arabes*, p. 58.

36. Ibid., p. 42.

37. Clancy-Smith, "La Femme Arabe," p. 63.

38. Ibid.

39. Cited in Thomas Deltombe, *L'Islam imaginaire: La construction médiatique de l'islamophobie en France, 1975 2005* (Paris: La Découverte, 2005), p. 232.

40. Hal Lehrman, "The Battle of the Veil in Algeria," *New York Times Magazine*, July 13, 1958, p. 14. See also Todd Shepard, *The Invention of Decolonization: The Algerian War and the Remaking of France* (Ithaca: Cornell University Press, 2006), pp. 186–92.

41. Frantz Fanon, *A Dying Colonialism*, trans. Haakon Chevalier (New York: Grove Press, 1965), p. 47.

42. Ibid., p. 63.

43. Ibid., p. 57.

44. Ibid., p. 52.

45. Ibid., p. 61.

46. David C. Gordon, *Women of Algeria: An Essay on Change* (Cambridge, Mass.: Harvard University Press, 1968), p. 55. See also Shepard, *The Invention of Decolonization*, chapter 7.

47. Fanon, *Dying Colonialism*, p. 44.

48. Gordon, *Women of Algeria*, p. 62.

49. Pierre Bourdieu, preface to Abdel Sayad, *L'immigration ou les paradoxes de l'alterité* (Paris and Brussels: De Boeck and Larcier, 1991), p. 9. I am grateful to Sylvia Schafer for calling this to my attention.

50. Citations in Françoise Gaspard and Claude Servan-Schreiber, *La fin des immigrés* (Paris: Seuil, 1984), p. 70.

51. Deltombe, *L'Islam imaginaire*, p. 253.

52. Ibid., p. 304.

53. Pierre Tevanian, *Le voile médiatique: Un faux débat: "l'affaire du foulard islamique"* (Paris: Editions Raisons d'agir, 2005), p. 112.

54. Ibid., p. 113.

55. Ibid., p. 114.

56. *Le Figaro*, October 24, 1989.

57. Cited in Esther Benbassa, *The Jews of France: A History from Antiquity to the Present*, trans. M. B. DeBevoise (Princeton: Princeton University Press, 1999), p. 81.

58. Ibid., p. 118.

59. Ibid., p. 169.

60. Ibid., p. 199.

61. Deltombe, *L' Islam imaginaire*, p. 65.

62. Adrien Favell, *Philosophies of Integration: Immigration and the Idea of Citizenship in France and Britain* (New York: Palgrave, 2001), p. 70.

63. Deltombe, *L' Islam imaginaire*, p. 66.

64. Ibid., p. 231.

65. Ibid., p. 347.

66. Tevanian, *Le voile médiatique*, p. 114.

67. Ibid., 114–15.

68. See Tom Charbit, *Les harkis* (Paris: La Découverte, 2006).

69. Loi no. 2005-158, *Journal Officiel*, no. 46 (February 24, 2005): 3128. The text can be found online at http://www.assemblée-nationale.fr/12/dossiers/rapataries.asp.

70. Jean-Pierre Thibaudat, "Des historiens s'élèvent contre un article de la loi sur les harkis," *Libération*, March 26, 2005.

3. Secularism

1. Debré, *La laïcité à l'école*, vol. 1, p. 12.

2. William E. Connolly, *Why I Am Not a Secularist* (Minneapolis: University of Minnesota Press, 1999), p. 153.

3. Slavoj Žižek, "For a Leftist Appropriation of the European Legacy," *Journal of Political Ideologies*, February 1998.

4. Stasi, *Laïcité et République*.

5. Jean-Dominique Bridienne, "Les droits, la tolérance et la laïcité," *Education et Pédagogies* 7 (September 1990).

6. Jean Baubérot, "La République et la laïcité: Entretien avec Jean Baubérot," *Regards sur l'Actualité*, no. 298 (February 2004), p. 14.

7. The classic description of this is Eugen Weber's, *Peasants into Frenchmen: The Modernization of Rural France 1870–1914* (Stanford: Stanford University Press, 1976). James Lehning's *Peasant and French: Cultural Contact in Rural France during the Nineteenth Century* (Cambridge: Cambridge University Press, 1995) offers the revisionist interpretation.

8. Stasi, *Laïcité et République*, p. 138; and Debré, *La laïcité à l'école*, vol. 1, p. 45, citing Jacques Chirac at Valenciennes, October 21, 2003: "La laïcité n'est pas négociable."

9. Stasi, *Laïcité et République*, p. 13.

10. Ibid., p. 36.

11. For earlier examples of this reasoning, see François Goguel (1990), in *Laïcité française*, vol. 1. In the same source, see also Jean-Dominique Bridienne (1990), "Les droits, la tolérance et la laïcité."

12. *Libération*, October 20, 1994. On these and other contradictions, see also Etienne Balibar, "Dissonances dans la laïcité," in Charlotte Nordmann, ed., *Le foulard islamique en questions* (Paris: Editions Amsterdam, 2004), pp. 15–27.

13. Bertrand Ogilvie, "Laïcité comme temporalité," in Nordmann, *Le foulard islamique*, p. 100.

14. Jean Baubérot, "The Two Thresholds of Laicization," in Rajeev Bhargava, ed., *Secularism and Its Critics* (Oxford: Oxford University Press, 1998), p. 135.

15. Ibid., p. 124.

16. The entire text with additional commentary is reproduced in *ProChoix*, no. 25 (Summer 2003), pp. 14–15.

17. Elisabeth Roudinesco, *Libération*, May 27, 2003.

18. François Dubet, "La laïcité dans les mutations de l'école," in Michel Wieviorka, ed., *Une société fragmentée? Le multiculturalisme en débat* (Paris: La Découverte, 1997), pp. 85–172.

19. Ibid., p. 91.

20. Timothy B. Smith, *France in Crisis: Welfare, Inequality and Globalization since 1980* (Cambridge: Cambridge University Press, 2004), p. 199.

21. Dubet, "La laïcité dans les mutations," p. 97.

22. Ibid.

23. Cardinal Jean-Marie Lustiger in an interview with Agence France Presse, October 19, 1989. See also, Debré, *La laïcité à l'école*, vol. 1, pp. 52–53, and vol. 2, p. 245.

24. Balibar, "Dissonances," p. 26.

25. Bridenne, "Les droits," p. 56.

26. Debré, *La laïcité à l'école*, vol. 1, p. 42.

27. Joan Wallach Scott, *Parité! Sexual Equality and the Crisis of French Universalism* (Chicago: University of Chicago Press, 2005).

28. Emmanuel Terray, "L'hystérie politique," in Nordmann, *Le foulard islamique*, pp. 103–17.

29. Baubérot, "The Two Thresholds," p. 125.

30. Ibid., p. 126.

31. Ibid., pp. 135–36.

4. Individualism

1. Michael Sandel, "Religious Liberty: Freedom of Choice or Freedom of Conscience," in Bhargava, *Secularism and Its Critics*, p. 87.

2. Lévy, *Des filles comme les autres*, p. 63.

3. Roy, *Globalized Islam*, p. 6.

4. Saba Mahmood, "Feminist Theory, Embodiment, and the Docile Agent: Some Reflections on the Egyptian Islamic Revival," *Cultural Anthropology* 6, no. 2 (2001), pp. 215, 214.

5. Talal Asad, *Formations of the Secular: Christianity, Islam, Modernity* (Stanford: Stanford University Press, 2003), p. 197.

6. Cited in Terray, "L'hystérie politique," p. 113.

7. Debré, *La laïcité à l'école*, vol. 1, p. 77.

8. *Laïcité française*, vol. 1.

9. Stasi, *Laïcité et République*, p. 128.

10. Patrick Weil, "A Nation in Diversity: France, Muslims, and the Headscarf" (March 25, 2004), at www.openDemocracy.net.

11. Debré, *La laïcité à l'école*, vol. 1, pp. 103–4.

12. Ibid., vol. 1, p. 63.

13. Finkielkraut testimony to the Debré commission, cited in Aline Baïf, "Le débat sur la laïcité scolaire," *ProChoix*, nos. 26–27 (Autumn 2003), p. 89.

14. Cited in Charlotte Nordmann, "Le foulard islamique en questions," in Nordmann, *Le foulard islamique*, p. 166. On the issue of

rape, see also Caroline Fourest and Fiammetta Venner, "Les enjeux cachés du voile à l'école," *ProChoix*, no. 25 (Summer 2003), p. 27.

15. "Entretien avec Jacqueline Costa-Lascoux," *ProChoix*, no. 28 (Spring 2004), p. 60.

16. Deltombe, *L'Islam imaginaire*, p. 230.

17. *Le Figaro*, October 20, 1994.

18. Anne Vigerie and Anne Zelensky, "'Laïcardes' puisque féministes," *ProChoix*, no. 25 (Summer 2003), p. 12. Here I can't resist noting that this seems an all too literal illustration of French psychoanalyst Jacques Lacan's famous comment that "the phallus can only play its role as veiled." Jacques Lacan, "The Meaning of the Phallus," trans. Jacqueline Rose, in Juliet Mitchell and Jacqueline Rose, eds., *Feminine Sexuality: Jacques Lacan and the École Freudienne* (New York: W. W. Norton, 1982), p. 82. Slovenian philosopher and Lacanian Slavoj Žižek suggests that the Islamic veil obfuscates "not the feminine body hidden by it, but the INEXISTENCE of the feminine." The veil creates the illusion, he says, that there is some "feminine Truth." It is, of course, "the horrible truth of lie and deception." The lie and deception are the insistence that there is a feminine essence, prior to our constructions of it, when in fact there is not. Slavoj Žižek, "The Antinomies of Tolerant Reason," at http://lacan.com/zizarchives.htm.

19. Debré, *La laïcité à l'école*, vol. 1, p. 10.

20. Ibid., vol. 1, p. 115.

21. *Le Monde*, December 15, 2003.

22. Alain Lipietz, "Le débat sur le foulard," *ProChoix*, nos. 26–27 (Autumn 2003), pp. 125–26.

23. Dounia Bouzar and Saïda Kada, *L'une voilée, l'autre pas: Le témoinage de deux musulmanes françaises* (Paris: Albin Michel, 2003), pp. 92–93.

24. Chahla Chafiq and Farhad Khosrokhavar, *Femmes sous le voile face à la loi islamique* (Paris: Editions du Félin, 1995), p. 163.

25. *Le Monde*, December 4–5, 1994.

26. Farhad Khosrokhavar, "L'universel abstrait," in Wiervorka,

Une société fragmentée?; and Cécile Dumas, "Entretien avec Farhad Khosrokhavar," *ProChoix*, nos. 26–27 (Autumn 2003), pp. 131–32.

27. Charlotte Nordmann and Jérôme Vidal, "La République à l'épreuve des discriminations," in Nordmann, *Le foulard islamique*, p. 11.

28. Saba Mahmood, *Politics of Piety: The Islamic Revival and the Feminist Subject* (Princeton: Princeton University Press, 2005), p. 152.

29. Bouzar and Kada, *L'une voilée*, pp. 13, 16.

30. Mahmood, "Feminist Theory," p. 215.

31. Ibid., p. 25.

32. Lévy, *Des filles comme les autres*, p. 63.

33. *Le Monde*, December 18, 2003.

34. Bouzar and Kada, *L'une voilée*, p. 27.

35. Abdellah Hammoudi, *A Season in Mecca: Narrative of a Pilgrimage*, trans. Pascale Ghazaleh (New York: Hill and Wang, 2006), p. 275.

36. Bouzar and Kada, *L'une voilée*, p. 62.

37. Ibid., p. 76.

38. Ibid., p. 34.

39. Ibid., p. 58.

40. *Le Monde Magazine*, September 9, 2006, p. 25.

41. Ibid., p. 82.

42. Ibid., p. 202.

43. Bouzar and Kada, *L'une voilée*, p. 29.

44. Lévy, *Des filles comme les autres*, p. 193.

5. Sexuality

1. Sylvie Pierre-Brossolette, "Laïcité, le jeu de loi," *Figaro Magazine*, December 13, 2003; and "Les religions face à une nouvelle loi," *Le Monde*, December 15, 2003.

2. Hammoudi, *A Season in Mecca*, p. 42.

3. Mahmood, *Politics of Piety*, pp. 110–17.

4. Chafiq and Khosrokhavar, *Femmes sous le voile*, p. 145.

5. Debré, *La laïcité à l'école*, vol. 1, p. 77.

6. Ibid., vol. 2, p. 52.

7. Ibid., vol. 2, p. 44.

8. *ProChoix*, nos. 26–27 (Autumn 2003), pp. 103–4.

9. *ProChoix*, no. 28 (Spring 2004), p. 57.

10. *L'Express*, November 17, 1994.

11. Deltombe, *L'Islam imaginaire*, p. 347.

12. Fanon, *A Dying Colonialism*, pp. 43–44.

13. Mona Ozouf, *Les mots des femmes: Essai sur la singularité française* (Paris: Fayard, 1995).

14. *Le Monde*, October 17, 2003.

15. Charles Hirschkind and Saba Mahmood, "Feminism, the Taliban, and the Politics of Counter-Insurgency," *Anthropological Quarterly* 75, no. 2 (Spring 2002), pp. 352–53.

16. See Sarkozy's blog: http://www.sarkozyblog.com/2005/immigration-une-immigration-choisie/. I am grateful to Eric Fassin for this reference. See his "La démocratie sexuelle et le conflit des civilisations," *Multitudes*, no. 26 (Fall 2006), pp. 123–31.

17. *Le Monde*, December 16, 2003.

18. Deltombe, *L'Islam imaginaire*, p. 352.

19. Christine Delphy, "Une affaire française," in Nordmann, *Le foulard islamique*, pp. 64–71.

20. Nacira Guénif-Souliamas and Eric Macé, *Les féministes et le garçon arabe* (Paris: Editions de l'Aube, 2004), p. 9.

21. Bouzar and Kada, *L'une voilée*, pp. 58–59.

22. Deltombe, *L'Islam imaginaire*, p. 70.

23. Ibid., p. 65.

24. Debré, *La laïcité à l'école*, vol. 2, p. 53.

25. Stasi, *Laïcité et République*, p. 114.

26. Ozouf, *Les mots des femmes*, p. 395.

27. Hammoudi, *A Season in Mecca*, p. 195.

28. Delphy, "Une affaire française," p. 64.

Conclusion

1. Caroline Fourest, *La tentation obscurantiste* (Paris: Grasset, 2005).

2. Fourest and Venner, "Les enjeux cachés du voile à l'école," p. 19.

3. Ibid., p. 31.

4. All of these quotes come from Pascale Krémer, "Paroles de françaises musulmanes: Les volontaires du voile," *Le Monde Magazine*, September 9, 2006, pp. 18–25.

5. Nordmann and Vidal, "La république à l'épreuve des discriminations," p. 7.

6. Danielle S. Allen, *Talking to Strangers: Anxieties of Citizenship after Brown vs. Board of Education* (Chicago: University of Chicago Press, 2004), pp. 85, 88, 91.

INDEX

abstraction, in politics, 13, 117, 168–69
affaire du string. See string (thong)
affaires des foulards, 21. *See also* head-scarf ban
affirmative action, 118
Algeria: agriculture in, 47; citizenship rights in, 48–49; "civilizing" of, 46–47, 54; civil war in, 27, 67, 72; colonialism and, 45–54, 85–86; French attitude toward, 27, 41; immigrants from, 50–52, 68; post-independence, 42–43; war (1954–1962) in, 61–67, 136; women in, 160
Allen, Danielle, 182
Alloula, Malek, 56, 58
anti-Semitism, 76–79
Arabs: Berbers versus, 48; "civilizing" of, 46–47, 49–50, 54, 68, 81, 84–85, 89; community among, 53; French studies of, 49; Muslims conflated with, 17, 26, 44, 46; racism toward, 42–46, 49–52; sexuality of, 52, 56–59, 71, 130; stereotypes of, 45, 49, 52, 56–58,

69, 71, 130; women, as represented by French, 54–60
Asad, Talal, 128, 141
assimilation: colonialism and, 46; criticisms of, 104; difference and, 19; of immigrants, 53, 79; of Jews, 75–76; models of, 147; of Muslims, 7–8, 75, 135, 173–74; schools and, 99; universalism and, 12–13. *See also* integration
Auclert, Hubertine, 57–59

Badinter, Elisabeth, 85
Balibar, Etienne, 114–15, 177, 182
Balladur, Édouard, 186n7
Battle of Algiers, The (film), 65
Baubérot, Jean, 121–23, 177, 182
Bayrou, François, 27–28, 38, 103
Benbassa, Esther, 76–79
Berbers, 48
Bourdieu, Pierre, 68
Bouzar, Dounia, 138, 145–47, 164–66
Brown, Wendy, 19
Bugeaud (general), 55, 84

war against terrorism, 9
Weil, Patrick, 131
West, Islam versus, 9, 19, 74, 85
Why I Am Not a Secularist (Connolly), 93
women: Algerian, 160; Algerian War and, 61–67; colonialism and, 54–60, 160; essence of, 194n18; in France, 155–56; Iranian Revolution and, 70; Islam and status of, 4, 32–33, 130, 155; Muslim versus French, 162; in politics, 13, 70, 156, 164, 169–70; schools and, 107; sexuality and, 158, 170; stereotypes of, 57–58; as victims of Muslim patriarchy, 33, 58, 71, 107, 125–27, 129–31, 133, 145, 164. *See also* feminism

yarmulkes, 1, 35, 78, 107, 127, 128, 134, 186n7

Zanoun, Nadia, 138–39
ZEPs, 110, 113–14
Žižek, Slavoj, 93–94, 194n18

THE PUBLIC SQUARE BOOK SERIES
PRINCETON UNIVERSITY PRESS

Ruth O'Brien, Series Editor

Uncouth Nation: Why Europe Dislikes America by Andrei S. Markovits

The Politics of the Veil by Joan Wallach Scott

Hidden in Plain Sight: The Tragedy of Children's Rights from Ben Franklin to Lionel Tate by Barbara Bennett Woodhouse

The Case for Big Government by Jeff Madrick

The Posthuman Dada Guide: tzara and lenin play chess by Andrei Codrescu

Not for Profit: Why Democracy Needs the Humanities by Martha C. Nussbaum

With Thanks to the Donors of the Public Square

PRESIDENT WILLIAM P. KELLY,
THE CUNY GRADUATE CENTER

PRESIDENT JEREMY TRAVIS,
JOHN JAY COLLEGE OF CRIMINAL JUSTICE

MYRON S. GLUCKSMAN

CAROLINE URVATER